GO FISHING FOR

CARP

GO FISHING FOR
CARP

GRAEME PULLEN

The Oxford Illustrated Press

© 1990, Graeme Pullen
ISBN 1 85509 212 3

Published by:
The Oxford Illustrated Press, Haynes Publishing Group, Sparkford,
Nr Yeovil, Somerset BA22 7JJ, England.

Printed in England by:
J.H. Haynes & Co Limited, Sparkford, Nr Yeovil, Somerset.

British Library Cataloguing in Publication Data:
  Pullen, Graeme
    Go fishing for carp. - (Go fishing for)
    1. Carp fishing
    I. Title II. Series
    799.1752

    ISBN 1-85509-212-3

Library of Congress Catalogue Card Number:
  90-81556

All photos by the author.

Contents

Bubblers
Mudding
Boiling
Bow-Waving
Circlers
Margin Cruisers
Reed Knockers

Floatfishing
Bottom Fishing
Freelining
Ledgering
Floater Fishing

Bread
Worms
Casters
Maggots
Paste Baits
Seed Baits
Boilies
Nuts and Seeds
Floaters

Rods
Reels
Hooks
Nets
Miscellaneous Equipment

Dedication

There will only ever be one carp angler,
Richard Walker.
There will only ever be one carp,
44 lb Redmire Pool, 1952.

Introduction

If there is one species that stands out for attracting a dedicated group of followers in a relatively short period of time, it is the carp. Over the last thirty years, the interest shown by anglers in this fish has been quite remarkable, resulting in significant advances in the type of tackle available, methods of fishing and the distribution of the species. Once bitten by the carp bug, many anglers never fish for anything else which is perhaps a shame, but it is an indication of the great pleasure gained from carp fishing. Of all the coarse fish species, I have to admit that I sometimes think the carp possesses a knowledge and reasoning power beyond the scope of many anglers!

There are many in the fishing world who actually do not like carp, or carp fishermen. They feel the species is given too much prominence in the media — notably the angling press — and they dislike waters that are reserved exclusively for carp fishing. I love hooking a carp, but, while I have a great admiration for the cunning of the species, I do recognise their limitations. As a friend once said to me, "If the carp had the brains carp anglers think they have, the fish would be fishing for us instead!" Point taken.

As for carp monopolising some venues, this may well be true in certain cases but in general it is not done to the detriment of all other species, as some people seem to think. I know many excellent carp waters where several species co-exist quite harmoniously, all reaching creditable weights and breeding satisfactorily. Occasionally a group of like-minded carp enthusiasts get together and form a syndicate and then bid for the rental or outright purchase of a lake

Introduction

Carp — whatever size, they represent a great fighting fish for the beginner and experienced alike.

or similar area of water. Obviously in these cases carp will take precedence over other fish, but angling clubs are always free to compete for the acquisition of such waters. Invariably these privately-run carp waters are well maintained and fish stocks and water conditions are constantly monitored — all of which must surely help to make a worthwhile fishery.

Since the early 1980s there has been a trend amongst carp fishermen to concentrate almost exclusively on catching the largest carp available rather than just enjoying fishing for any carp swimming the waters. It is quite strange the way the popularity of this fish has rocketed in just thirty years, for of course the carp has been with us for centuries. The species originates from Asia, in the Caspian and Black Seas and as far afield as Burma, Russia and

Go Fishing for Carp

Over 50 lb, this monster carp came from South Africa. Today, the specialist carp angler is prepared to travel abroad to find the truly monster carp. Fish to over 50 lb are likely in the more prolific foreign waters.

China. The farthest east I have caught them is Greece and the farthest west, Arizona, USA. Moving south, I have caught them in the Natal region of South Africa, but looking north I'm afraid the furthest I can claim to have caught them is south of Watford!

For the most part the carp is a sedentary fish, quite happy to localise itself in certain areas of a lake or river. Yet around the Volga Delta in Russia the fish have been known to migrate to the sea. I imagine this largely depends on the salinity of the water, a large amount of freshwater being flushed downriver. From Europe to the Middle East the carp's status as a sportfish is minimal, and almost all fish bred commercially are done so for food. This strikes a note of outrage in the hearts of our dedicated carp anglers, and the thought of a plate of fried carp on a bed of rice is almost more than they can bear. For the inhabitants of those countries, however, carp may form a large part of their staple diet.

Many of our own carp originate from the commercially bred 'farmed' fish, imported on account of their ability to grow quickly. The common carp is not native to Britain but was thought to have been introduced by our monasteries to supplement their food when

Introduction

times were hard. The carp held in the monastery stock lakes for fattening are now known as wild carp and they put up a tremendous scrap when hooked. The first carp I ever caught was in fact a wild carp of 5 lb, taken from a lake near my home known to be used by monks in the dim and distant past.

The recent surge in interest in carp fishing can almost entirely be attributed to one man, Richard Walker. In 1952 he broke the British Carp record by an enormous margin, eclipsing the British record held by Albert Buckley, from Mapperley Reservoir, which then stood at 26 lb. Walker's fish, taken from the famed Redmire Pool, scaled a massive 44 lb. The magnificent fish was named Clarissa, and was reputed to be 15 years old at capture. It lived for a further 18 years in an aquarium at London Zoo giving many the chance to see the biggest carp ever landed on rod and line in Britain.

Nothing quite like it had ever happened in the fishing world before. The vast majority of anglers regarded carp as uncatchable and any contact that did result in a fish in the net was regarded as something of a fluke. But there was no fluke about Richard Walker's fish. He had tamed several other big carp before his record capture, and as an angler wanting to learn more, he began evolving new techniques, theories and tackle that proved to be the foundation of carp fishing as we know it today. I am sure he did not realise the significance of not only his massive catch, but also his writings in the angling press that so many anglers, myself included, have held on to. Walker himself turned his attention to other species but those who read of his exploits and adopted his ideas also began to enjoy success and to catch carp — big carp regularly.

The carp is a tremendous scrapper, digging into weedbeds, boring through lily pads and straining every item of tackle (and the angler's nerves!) as it heads for the sanctuary of the snags. To wait expectantly for hours, or sometimes days and then nights, and then to finally hook a fish only to watch it bore straight into a snag without any effort, and break the line in the process, is quite heart-rending. It has happened to me so I know what it's like!

Another equally frustrating experience is to watch a shoal, or a single fish, cruise over your baited area in the last fading hours of daylight. You wait, often staying awake all night . . . and nothing happens. The dawn sun burns brightly and you peer into your swim. All the bait has gone, yet there was no registration of a bite. Infuriated and humiliated, you head for home.

Alternatively, imagine yourself sitting in the branches of a comfortable tree above a lake one fine day in July, when the weeds have grown up. The surface of the lake is dimpled with a carpet of floating food particles and a fish has already started to take some. You scatter more feed and then send in your bait with a hook hidden it, losing it well amongst the other particles. Gradually the carp moves closer, slowly slurping down the loose samples, unworried, calm. As the samples are depleted, the carp makes for your patch and starts to suck down the surrounding particles. Five, four, three are left. Then a slight pause and the third and second have gone too. Tipping its head towards the hook-bait, something clicks in that fishy head and it bolts away, leaving the water boiling on the surface. How does it know? You haven't moved, you've barely breathed. That, my friend, is what makes carp fishing exciting!

In contrast I feel I should mention a style of carp fishing that has

The author sizes up a gravel pit prior to baiting up. Winter can be a difficult time for location, but it is made easier by the fact that the carp, once located are rarely likely to move far.

been — perhaps quite rightly — ridiculed by anglers after other species. This carp angler casts into a heavily prebaited swim using three rods, sometimes more. This terminal gear is self-hooking (known as a 'bolt-rig'). He sleeps in a comfortable, thermally-insulated sleeping bag, on a customised bed-chair under a large canvas bivouac. In some extreme cases he equips himself with full cooking facilities and a portable television powered by a car battery. He cooks a meal, does the washing up, watches television and then settles down for a comfortable night's sleep — just like home. The fish, should it take, hooks itself, and the angler is made aware of the event by a specially toned bite indicator. He climbs out of bed and picks up the rod, the reel already yielding line before he does so. Of course technically it is still carp fishing, but it hardly matches up to the traditional methods of even thirty years ago.

Returning a double-figure carp. Hold the fish upright in the water, gently lowering it beneath the surface until the gills are covered. Do not push the fish away, wait until it is strong enough to move off by itself.

Go Fishing for Carp

There are still many anglers, however, who enjoy the traditional methods of striking their own fish and who are not totally preoccupied with the size of the carp as long as they get good sport. This book is written for them, as well as for all the newcomers to the sport with a similar attitude. Don't worry about trying to break the British record—you will soon become disillusioned. (The frequent advertisements for second-hand carp tackle in the angling press bear witness to the fact that many have started off with this intention.) Accept the carp for what he is, a fine sporting fish whatever its size.

About the Species

Having given the carp a brief introduction I should mention the different varieties of carp that might find their way into your net — the common, mirror, grass, ornamental, linear, leather, wildie or crucian carp. Many years ago the biggest carp was referred to as a 'King', but that name has fallen out of fashion and nowadays it is known as a common carp. The fish are all basically similar in appearance, their colours changing with their habitat, and their outlines changing according to the particular strain of fish. The true carp, or rather the first naturalised fish, is the **wildie** and it is this one that was stocked in the monastery lakes as an additional source of food for the monks. These fish are long and lean, with large evenly-marked scales covering their brassy sides and often a large head tapering down gradually towards their tails.

The wild carp is one of the smaller strains of carp and was originally thought to have little chance of exceeding a double figure weight. I know that is not true as I have seen fish run into double figures at one of my local ex-monastery lakes, and 9 pounders are taken each season. I have also read of a 20 lb 3 oz wild carp being landed in Edwardian times, but have never heard it confirmed. Wildies are slow growers and are seldom sought after by angling clubs for stocking purposes. They are often, however, the target of carp anglers who want to be able to say they have landed every variety of carp in the British Isles.

The wildies I used to catch as a youngster all took either bread-flake or crust on the surface, or freelined par-boiled potato. The

15

Go Fishing for Carp

This angler looks delighted with his catch of wild carp, taken from a lake on a private estate, which used to be a home to the monks.

field at the back of the lake where we fished just happened to be a potato field, and in the evenings we would sneak off, dig up some spuds, put them on the stove, eat as many as we could with baked beans, and use the rest for bait! Those wildies could have been netted out in late May when they swam in inches of water during spawning. In fact a local carp farm owner used to come down and scrape all the eggs off the weed, take them back and try to hatch them out but I believe he only had limited success. I would venture to suggest that most anglers would have little chance of catching a real wild carp today as so many waters have been taken over and stocked with farm-reared fish that most are now a result of cross

16

breeding. Wildies respond very well to particle baits like corn, and baked beans, especially when fished on light link ledger rigs, 5-lb line and Avon rods more suited to barbel. Many ex-monastery estate lakes are very shallow which possibly accounts for the wildies turn of speed when hooked. They are fun to fish and if you ever get the chance to fish for them, take it.

My first encounter with a wildie came when I was about 13 or 14. A friend and I spent an afternoon heaving bowls full of mashed bread and bran off a bridge that ran over a section of the lake. We had intended to fish the following night, but on arrival, we found two tents pitched on the bridge with other youngsters set up in our swims. That was my first encounter with 'swim poachers', as nobody in their right mind would think of pitching tents and fishing from a bridge! It later transpired on the school grapevine that they had watched us from bushes but I have to admit that I had the last laugh. I crawled over, under cover of darkness, and unscrewed the nut on their "Heron" buzzers so that the contacts wouldn't register a bite! During the night I had several runs on breadflake, and stood in the darkness with line trickling from the spool as I misguidedly waited for the carp to "turn the bait"! I had obviously read too many pike articles, and couldn't understand why those carp didn't stop running to "turn the bait". Eventually I whacked one, and landed a 5 pounder, which was indeed my first ever carp.

Mention should perhaps also be made of the **grass** carp, an oriental species that has been introduced with some success on a few venues to try to control weed growth, this being the species', main diet. There was a lot of resistance to the introduction of this species in a number of areas as it was thought that an "alien" species might have a detrimental effect on the rest of the fishery. However, it appears they are doing the job of weed clearing well, and have now been stocked in a few selective waters. They are also long in shape, with a smaller mouth than the mirrors or common carp and — not unlike a cross between a chub and a wild carp. I believe they will be a species to look out for in future years. They may certainly represent some interesting new bait theories.

The common, mirror and leather carp are all strains of the king carp, and have been bred by the commercial carp farmer, generally

Go Fishing for Carp

The wild carp. A long lean body with a large head. Originally thought to be distributed as a food fish by monasteries, the wild carp is becoming increasingly rare as fishing clubs take over more estate waters.

on the continent. The **common** carp used to be particularly in vogue in the Seventies when every carp angler wanted to catch the biggest common carp available. They are beautifully shaped fish with long bodies and even scales covering their entire flanks. The leather carp, for instance, with its lack of scales was bred for its ease of cleaning on the kitchen table. The fully-scaled commons were not so popular as scales flew all over the place when they were scraped off! The commons, to my mind, are far more uniform in appearance than the leathers or mirrors. Both of these tend to come from the faster growing strains and, depending on the amount of food in the water, their belly girth can grow faster than their spine. This results in those fat, blobby, football-shaped fish that from their length should weigh about 5 lb, but on the scales weigh about 13 lb! Some can also become very hump backed with a small head and small tail fin.

These fast growers form the mainstay of our 8 to 25-lb fish range today. While some angling clubs will buy in carp in the fingerling size to stock and grow on at their own rate, others want instant big

About the Species

The common carp. The regular-size smaller scales completely cover the flanks, giving a burnished metal effect.

fish and buy in double-figure fish, or larger, straight from a stockist. Carp are a tough species, and providing they have a basic food supply they will survive and, conditions permitting, multiply fairly rapidly. Their main food is the bloodworm, found in the soft mud on the bottom of lakes. The carp eats the bloodworm, which is a midge larva, like soup. It buries its nose into the mud, sucks up a mouthful, puffs the unwanted mud out through its gills or passes it straight through its digestive system and extracts the food. Larger items such as shrimps and snails are also eaten, but these will be crushed smaller by the pharyngeal, or throat teeth first.

The carp is a member of the cyprinid family, all of which have toothless jaws. They grind their food up using pharyngeal teeth, mashing the food against a bony plate. With this sort of digestive system they have to eat little and often, in contrast to predators that can feed well and then not eat for several days while they digest the food. With these throat teeth, the carp can crush up mussel shells, ejecting the shells and eating the meat. Try observing their feeding

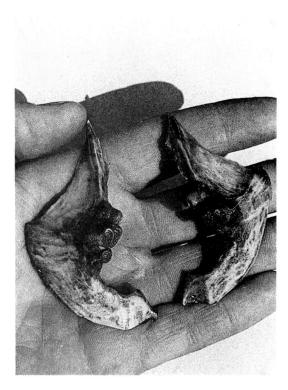

This picture shows the remarkably large set of pharangeal or throat teeth from a 37-lb Hampshire carp. These are used by all species of cyprinidae fish for crushing their food. Hence their need to feed on the little-and-often basis.

techniques through aquariums; I have learnt some very interesting feeding habits that way.

The **mirror** carp has some scales but they vary in size (though they are generally large), and they are scattered over the flanks and back. A rarer fish is the fully-scaled mirror carp, which is covered with scales and looks like the common carp but the scales are much larger. As a semi-scaleless fish the mirror carp was presumably reared for easy preparation in the kitchen but it is rated highly in the breeders' books too.

The **leather** carp is the housewife's dream — no scales at all, just a smooth, leathery skin. A compromise between the mirror and leather is the linear carp. This is best described as a leather carp but it has a uniform strip of big scales running along the lateral line and back. I have also heard it referred to as a saddleback, but to my

The rarer fully-scaled mirror carp, with large scales completely covering its flanks.

Profile of a mirror carp, with a few large scales scattered over its flank.

Originally bred as an easy-to-clean table fish, the leather carp has no scales at all.

The author with a raggety-tail double-figure mirror carp. The fins can be treated to prevent further damage, with water resistant antiseptics.

mind the true saddleback has no scales along the lateral line, just along the back.

There may also be a limited number of **ornamental** carp in a few waters, and I have seen some small Kois in some waters. They wobble their way along just under the surface. At weights of a pound or so they hardly represent a serious angling proposition, but they are another variety of carp to add to your collection if you are that way inclined. There is also an ornamental carp known as the golden carp which was bred primarily for display in estate ponds. It doesn't have the ordinary colour pigmentation under its skin but instead has a beautiful golden hue. In a natural environment it would undoubtedly attract attention from all sorts of predators, including the heron. The only real chance of coming into contact with one would be if someone introduced the odd one or two into a fishery. I have heard of Koi carp being stocked in small fisheries partly as a commercial venture, and partly to give anglers some sport. Knowing the extortionate price that Kois fetch on the open market, I cannot imagine they would remain in the water for very long!

All varieties of carp are prolific breeders, especially the smaller **crucian**. Like the larger carp the crucian was not a native British fish, but introduced from Asia sometime around the seventeenth century. It is a fine sporting fish on light tackle, renowned for its dogged tug-tug fight as it turns its broad flank away from the pull of the rod. It was stocked after the bigger King carp (which gave us the commons, mirrors, leathers etc), and has been made more popular by angling clubs who find that this particular species has an affinity for coloured weedy waters where they thrive and multiply. They are also free biters so give the angler plenty of action, even during the hot, bright summer afternoons when everything else has long gone.

It is a non-migratory species, and generally stays wherever the food and environment suits it best. It was originally bred for ornamental ponds, but its fast growth rate quickly ensured it went to the top of the list of clubs with restocking programmes. Many angling clubs have a thriving match section and it is here that the popularity of crucian fishing comes into its own. The "serious" big carp man however, will not want to read about, or even get bites from crucians, but this is a carp book written for anglers willing to catch all species of carp, so I feel it worthwhile to include a small section on how to catch crucians later in the book.

The small commons and large crucians are often mistaken for the same fish. Once you see the two side by side, however, you can see they are totally different. Both varieties have a long tapering dorsal fin, and both are covered uniformly by even scales. But in the crucian the leading tip of the dorsal is rounded, and the body is far more hump backed. You can also tell them apart by fin ray counts, but I don't think the angler will need to go to this length. The tell-tale sign of the crucian is the lack of barbules around the mouth, although I have caught hybrids between the two that make you think you are looking at an enormous crucian, when in fact the strain is probably more common carp.

Crucians have a beautiful gold colour blending to dark olive on the back, and with a goldy bronze sheen to the scales. They have an off-white or cream belly, as opposed to the white of other carp. They seem to thrive everywhere except in fast rivers. Deep gravel pits, estate lakes, stagnant ponds, canals and slow moving rivers all support this scrappy little sportster. The weedier the water the better, as they feed around and amongst the roots and stems of all weeds. They also spawn in the same area, leaving their eggs adhering to the stems of aquatic plants. Prime months for spawning are May and June, but it can be later if a bad winter has been followed by a particularly cold spring.

The fish is said to keep well out of water, and has even been thought to stay alive in the mud of ponds that have partially dried out. Their metabolism certainly seems to adapt to warm water and low oxygen levels better than other members of the cyprinid family. Having established that the fish is basically small, an average national size might be about twelve ounces. Two pounds is a very nice fish, and it may reach a weight in excess of six or seven pounds. In a rich water they can pack on weight quicker than most species I know. Not only are they popular with the match and pleasure angler, but pike place them high on their menu also. Find a water that has had a recent introduction of crucians, and you will find a couple of years after stocking that the pike fishing is very good. Crucians are generally top of the pike angler's livebait list, although I refuse to use them, as they are such a grand fish for the young and beginner angler, that they deserve a better fate than to be dished up to a pike. I will use anything else, but not the chunky little crucians.

The bigger mirror and leather carp are also prolific breeders, with spawning taking place from May to July generally in shallow, weedy water. Any angler fish-spotting around the margins of his local fishery on a hot summer's day in the close season will be amazed at how close the carp spawn to the bank. Like the bream, the carp develops a rough patch on its forehead during spawning that is called a tubercule. The female can lay an enormous number of eggs, running into tens of thousands, but the mortality rate can be high. Eels, water fowl and drought can take their toll, and I believe the fertiliser run off into some carp waters stops many eggs hatching properly as well. That is why some good carp waters hold only the stock originally put in, not thousands of smaller carp that would be their progeny.

On waters that do allow the young to develop quickly, and where the predator take is minimal, you will find tremendous sport on light match tackle with fish ranging from six ounces to around one pound in weight. They look beautiful, miniature replicas of the big fish, and usually fin-perfect. If you have a water with an abundance of this size carp, it is best to net most of them out, and sell or exchange them for other species within angling clubs otherwise you run the risk of developing only a stunted carp fishery.

Fishing for Crucian Carp

I feel this sporty little species deserves a section on its own. The traditional approach to the larger carp will be unsuccessful for crucians. Certainly they can be taken occasionally on particle baits, but if you approach them differently, in a way more suited to their size and habits, then not only will you enjoy your sport more, but your success rate will be greater.

Running up to a size in excess of five pounds, you can set yourself up for either bags of crucians under 1 lb, or set yourself a specimen target of, say, 2 lb. Although less than 50% of the British record, a 2-lb crucian is a good sporting proposition on light tackle, and worth the same as a 20-lb mirror carp. The best way to tackle the crucian is to find a water where the stocking was done within the last three years. In my own experience crucian fishing is great when you fish after the initial stocking has been done. Give them a year in a new water, and they quickly settle down to feeding. This makes for comparatively easy fishing, but gives you experience on their bites. After about three years in a water they seem to thin out, and the bigger fish are more difficult to locate. I believe they lose the gullibility of youth, and even adopt an entirely different feeding pattern. Find a shoal of small crucians, set them up feeding confidently, and the world as they say, is your oyster. For building a good catch of crucian carp you need to maintain a good steady

26

Fishing for Crucian Carp

The crucian carp. A much chubbier species, without the four large barbules around the mouth.

stream of falling baits and feed through the surface layers. This species will feed all the way through the depth ranges from the surface to the lake bed, but once the feed is hard on the bottom, you can have trouble hitting bites. It's almost as though they become more cagey once the feed is on the bottom.

Far better to introduce a slow sinking cloud groundbait that falls in a puff of white, rather than a hard ball of groundbait that plummets to the bottom, and takes hours to break up. For that reason just dampen your groundbait, don't soak it, and mix in some sweet flavouring like strawberry or maple cream. To this mixture you should add some small feed like pinkies, and throw small balls in at regular intervals. I often throw out groundbait before I have even tackled up, as the crucians can move in on the feed while I set up.

For hookbaits use red maggots — one or two on a size 16 to 2-lb hook link. Floatfishing with a small waggler is all you want with the shot bulked under the float, and one dust shot about six inches from the hook. You want that hookbait to sink slowly, if possible through the other feed. Overcast your swim, wind back with the rod tip under water to sink the line, then throw in a golf-ball-size ball of groundbait. If you get the shoal of crucians feeding, the bites will be fast as the species seem to take the bait faster when higher in the water.

As the lakebed becomes carpeted with groundbait they get a bit full, and browse over the baited area feeding randomly rather than excitedly. I believe this accounts for the better bites when you first start fishing. Ease off with the groundbait if the bites slow, and then just catapult out loose red maggots to bring them off the bottom. I was once told the success of the red maggot was due to its similarity to a bloodworm, but surely the taste is what makes the fish eat a bait?

As for tackle, you can use a closed-faced match reel and a 13-foot match rod, or you can use a pole. The faster crucian fisherman will stick to the pole, and pop the fish out using 5-lb line straight through to a crook, rather than a weaker hooklink and pole elastic as shock absorber. The fish will dictate what you use in the way of hooklink, and once you start hitting crucians near the pound mark, they will be too strong to swing in with crook and 5-lb line. Other baits to try are hemp and caster, feeding the hemp and using caster on the hook. I never mind using a caster that has gone slightly darker towards the 'floater' stage, as the dust shot will counteract this and make the bait sink even slower. Plain white maggots are fine, but only last for a short period before the bites die off. Red are better, and bronze can be used in the winter. If you want to build a good catch of crucians always net them if using light line rather than trying to swing them to hand. This little scrapper has a very characteristic jag-jag-jag fight on your rod tip, and often they dig deep near the net.

The bigger fish you need to approach almost like mini-carp. Forget the lighter feed and red maggots. Fish like that and you get the small ones coming which in turn might alarm any larger fish. Select a swim on the fringe of a weedbed, away from the known areas of the small crucians. Put in no groundbait as this attracts small fry, and in turn attracts the small crucians. Use a bigger loose feed like sweetcorn, which if you use a couple of grains on a size 12 hook should eliminate bites from smaller fish. Crucians of 2 lb and over can be taken on the float, but I have had more success by fishing hard on the bottom for them. In contrast to small crucians the bites seem more confident with a ledgered bait, so to that end use a light weight like a link-ledger with just a single swan shot as weight. Again, overcast the baited swim, but allow the line to tighten as much as possible before putting on the bobbin indicator. This should be a light piece of plastic, or even roll of silver paper.

The bigger crucian will often play with bait, spitting it out several times before moving off with it. Strike only when you get a confident take on the bobbin. Hook links can still be around 2 lb, and the match rod and reel still employed, but ensure any plastic ledger stop you use is pinched onto the main line, not the hook link. Keep scattering half a dozen grains of corn into the swim every fifteen minutes, and occasionally feed with corn, but scale down the hook size to 16 and try caster on the hook. If you get small crucian go straight back to a size 12 and double grains of corn.

On many big carp waters the crucians have taken to nibbling

A crucian with a touch of common in its breeding. Not all hybrids are likely to have exactly the same characteristics.

away at big carp paste baits, leaving a hook lying on the bottom. The same doesn't apply to boilies which have a toughened skin, but paste baits will often pick up good crucians, especially in winter. I suffered a couple of seasons of continually twitchy indicators while after bigger carp. The bobbin would tweak about, then keep dropping down as the fish nibbled and nosed the bait towards me. Striking was a fruitless exercise, and only the occasional crucian was hooked after they had nibbled the baits away. If you wind in a freelined paste bait slowly you can inspect the damage and see the tiny nibble marks on the outside.

I overcame this problem by fishing a big paste ball squeezed around a link ledger. In place of the link ledger I put a plastic ledger stop with a heavy piece of 30-lb nylon threaded through it. This helped hook on the paste ball. I made the paste ball extra hard, fished it short, about six inches from the hook, and onto a size 12 hook, pinched a piece of paste just covering the hook. The idea was that the crucian would first take the paste without the hook, get confident and then take the other ball with the hook. This technique caught me a lot of bigger crucians. The only problem was when a big carp came along, ignored the small piece of paste and gulped down the whole paste ball without my hook in it! I lost a few good carp like that, but I had cracked the problem of the bigger crucians which was satisfying.

The crucian carp loves a weedy, coloured water, and when it is six to eight feet deep you can catch them during the brightest sunshine. Crucians have no barbules at the side of their mouths, but beware of the crucian common hybrid, as where the two species are found in abundance hybridisation does occur. They fight just as well, but you may have problems taking the club's specimen trophy with a hybrid. They are generally longer than the traditionally round crucian, and even if you have only caught nets of half pound true crucians, you will notice there is something different about the 2 or 3-lb "monster" lying in your net!

One of the best baits to fish on the bottom for big crucians is a fingernail-size piece of crust; this is especially useful for conditions where soft bottom weed exists. You can even lightly grease the hooklink with mucilin to slow its sinking rate so the bait rides above the weed. Some anglers dip the crust in a sweet flavouring before casting out. I prefer to use it unflavoured. Crucians in the larger sizes respond well to the swim-raking techniques used by tench fisherman. In fact they will often be in amongst the bait before the tench. Several times I have extracted a couple of good crucians on the first few casts into a newly dragged swim.

Floatfishing for crucians, especially when the bait is lying hard on the bottom, produces some strange bites. Sometimes the float can twiddle round in a circle and send ripples out, keeping you on the edge of your seat. Crucians don't drag or slide the float away gracefully like tench. One minute the float is twittering about in a strange manner, then just when you think a fish has left it, down she goes. The only reason I can think of for this is that the crucian, without the barbules of the larger carp, does not have the same sensation in its mouth. Maybe it sucks in a bait and spits it out several times before taking it. This seems to fit in with my theory already mentioned, of winter crucians and paste baits. They can be as finicky as the most hardened mirror carp, but the answer seems to be . . . let the bite progress.

The crucian carp will not be taken seriously by the big carp angler, yet size for size they are great scrappers. It is more the nature and activity of crucians that attracts me to them. You don't have to sit up three nights for a fish. Often those sublime summer evenings or crisp autumnal dawns are all you need to have some delightful fishing. Whether it's gravel pits, farm ponds, estate lakes, park lakes, moats or canals, a session after the crucian carp will make a lively change if you have been struggling with the big carp.

Habitat

Carp do well in almost all waters where there is a soft mud bottom. They can also grow very large in gravel pits, but those with a slight tinge of colour and plenty of soft bottom weed produce the fastest growers. Carp can adapt to anywhere where the temperature range is warm, and the food abundant; a couple of factors the carp angler would do well to remember in his search for fish. Some syndicated waters actually overstock above the normal accepted density per acre of carp. They put in more big fish than the natural food chain would allow to develop properly, then sustain this heavy stocking by feeding them artificially with a high-protein feed like trout pellets — especially during the cold winter months when natural food is at a minimum. The growth rate on these artificially fed fish can be enormous, much more than on naturally supported fish. Many anglers will not fish these waters, feeling they are too artificial, but although the fish are caught easily in the first week of the season, they soon learn to avoid the clumsy angler's approach, and are soon every bit as cagey as a naturally fed fish.

I cannot really see the difference myself, as once a carp has been stocked from a fish farm surely it is artificial anyway, and it doesn't matter if it is then fed on at the fishery. You then get drawn into the same argument as is waged between game fishermen when they discuss whether the naturalised British brown trout is better than the introduced rainbow trout. They are all fish, and still require catching!

Shallow, muddy lakes, with a deep central channel are great for

An ideal water for carp: some colour in the water to give them confidence, and plenty of weed to give them food and cover.

Surrey angler Mike Graham with a large carp that fell to chickpeas fished on a size 6 hook and 8-lb line.

Mudeford angler Neil Frances took this 19-lb 7-oz Mirror on a running lead rig, 11-lb line, with a dacron hook link terminating in a size 6 hook. Tiger nuts were the successful bait. Neil's best session at the Hampshire water was five fish on floater, including two twenty pounders.

Above: A tidy catch by any standard. Pole specialist Nigel Newport, the manager of "Tackle Up", netted over 55-lb of carp from MBK Leisure pits. Superb sport on light tackle.

Facing page: This Frensham Ponds common carp fell to a bolt rig fished at long distance. Note the green algal bloom that many anglers feel puts fish off. Much of the time it is only near the surface, and the bottom of the lake is still clear.

The author plays out a carp taken on floater. This can be a rewarding and entertaining way of picking up fish.

Above: Tranquil and serene. There is nothing like a session at a prolific carp lake when the conditions look right for a good catch.

Right: This is what happens when it all goes according to plan. This youngster took an amazing haul of three big doubles and a twenty pounder in one session at a Hampshire gravel pit.

Three of the more popular rigs for presenting a boilie bait to a carp. There are dozens of ways to rig baits for carp.

producing regular big fish. The shallows warm up quickly and induce them to feed as insect life is most prolific in warm mud. Then in very cold snaps when the shallow water cools off rapidly, the fish can move in to the deep channel, and will feed on the angler's bait also. Many of the day ticket and club waters today see an enormous influx of enthusiastic carp fishermen. Some of them put in an incredible amount of bait, both on the day of fishing and in the pre-baiting sessions. It is possible to put in too much bait. I have seen an angler wade out at one club water and catapult out an entire bucket of sweetcorn, which must have kept the carp occupied for days before they even came across his hookbait.

Reasonable intensive baiting, especially when high protein baits are used, help sustain a carp population in some fisheries. Without this extra bait some of the carp stocked would not only stop growing, but actually lose weight as well. My personal view is that prebaiting is fine on a syndicate water, or club water where you know who is putting in, how much, and of what bait. Unfortunately what happens on many carp waters is that angler number one comes, fires out his quotas of loose samples, hoping to fish the next night, then moves off. Half an hour later another angler, unaware of the baiting up of the first, moves in, wants to fish in two nights' time, so fires out a complete bucket of maple peas. He moves off. I then turn up, decide I only want to fish six hours, so fire out a couple of cans of sweetcorn. In that swim is enough bait for all the carp in the entire lake, and you run the risk of catching absolutely nothing as the swim goes sour with so much uneaten food in it!

This is a problem you cannot really solve as carp anglers are known to be very secretive about methods and baits, but the more successful are those that share their knowledge of which swim they are baiting, on which night, and with what bait. All this extensive baiting can also be mighty expensive, especially if you buy ready-made pre-packed baits from the tackle shops. Whilst it eliminates the need to spend hours concocting and mixing up your own baits, and you know a colouring and flavouring has been tried and tested on carp before, you pay a price for this convenience. Of ready-made baits the boilies are possibly the most successful, and you can read more on these in another of my books: *Freshwater Fishing Baits*.

Go Fishing for Carp

You might find it interesting.

The main problem that occurs with all carp fishing is that which arises when they start to feed heavily on the natural food in a very rich lake. When they feed on the bloodworm, with their noses sunk up to five inches in the mud, they cannot see the angler's bait. This means you can be fishing among feeding fish without getting any bites, except those that bump the line, and which are known as "liners".

This problem was solved to a certain extent by buoying up the bait to raise it just above the soft mud or bottom weed. The hope is that as the carp comes up for a "breather" he sees or smells the bait, thinking he has disturbed it by his rooting around and takes it. However pop-ups are also successful when fished over hard bottoms, so I think it is because you are isolating a bait and making it stand out among the others that makes them take it.

Where To Fish Carp

The carp, as previously mentioned, can exist virtually anywhere in the British Isles. Having said that, the best of the fishing is in England, with Wales, Scotland and Ireland having, on a broad basis, what I would describe as limited stocks. Having said that, I am well aware of a few waters where the stocking density is equal to that of many English waters, and this is especially true in Ireland, where the carp is sure to make an impact in the next decade or so. There are several waters there that first came to anglers' attention when the grapevine spoke of carp to double figures coming from them. Those waters are now throwing up twenty pounders and I feel sure that the massive expanse of waterways in Ireland, coupled with its very mild climate, will soon see carp well in excess of 30 lb.

Why the latter three places should not have such good fishing must surely be due to population density, or rather the lack of it, coupled to the fact that Wales, Scotland and Ireland are all premier game fish areas. The game fishes have doubtless put restrictions on the influx of carp because they might upset the ecological balance of the trout, although I suspect much stocking has already been done illegally by anglers wishing to see more waters with carp in them.

Habitat

Gravel Pits and Lakes

It has to be said that the gravel pits around central and southern England have now been accepted as possibly the finest carp fisheries in Britain. Most of these were created over the last twenty-five years when vast quantities of gravel were needed for the construction of the motorway systems around England. When flooded, the pits presented a whole new concept for carp fishing. The first ten years of a newly flooded pit is when it is at its richest, and those stocked immediately produced the first of the double-figure and twenty-pound carp. The motorway system also meant that carp enthusiasts could travel long distances quickly to put in many more short sessions and so boost their catch rate and knowledge.

Many of these pits are on angling schemes and can only be fished with a permit, usually for a season, from companies like Leisure

The author scours a water with binoculars in an effort to locate carp. Binoculars are useful on new waters of which you may have no previous experience. Bow-waves, bubbles and dorsal fins are all signs to look for.

Sport and Ameys. Without a doubt the gravel pits have now taken over from the traditional lake and pond systems in providing new waters for carp anglers. Not only did they present new water, but new techniques had to be applied to extract the carp. Many traditional estate lakes and angling club waters were of a consistent depth and with a soft mud bottom. The prevailing wind in this country is supposed to be a south-westerly, and this directional airflow causes the wave action that can move the softer silt towards one end of the lake. As a general rule therefore, the north of estate and open waters is deeper than the south. This is because the greatest wave action is concentrated at the northerly end during prevailing winds and this rocks away at the lighter silt, creating slightly deeper water.

In contrast, the gravel pits are all man made and not susceptible to wave action erosion as the base is gravel or gravel and clay. The bottom contour of such lakes in fact can alter drastically in even a couple of yards. This is due to the excavation technique used at the time called "throwback". It left the bed with undulates and valleys which create food traps for any feeding carp. Now the wave action can have an effect. Any action will wear away at the silt on the top of the "humps", because waves are stronger in shallow water than deep. This will expose the heavier stones which will not be moved by wave action, and create a gravel bar. Some of this silt in suspension will sink slowly down the side of the hill to come to rest in the "valleys". This gives a medium for weed to take hold and grow, and you then have a good place for carp to root around the bottom and feed. This is in the early life of a gravel pit —ossibly the first five to eight years after it has been stocked. The bankside is level, and therefore the wave action there will be at its greatest.

What happens next, is the bankside vegetation grows up of its own accord, or is planted as part of a landscaping scheme. As this vegetation increases it reduces the amount of wave action on the "humps" of those gravel bars. They become slightly silted. This allows finer weeds to grow, and of course being shallower the humps will warm up quicker in the sunshine hours. Therefore this is the place to fish for the carp. Of course the carp now have two feeding areas of soft mud and I cannot advise you which to fish, only that early gravel pits will have little food on the tops of the gravel bars, and you will do better to bait the dropoff or edge where it slopes away into deeper water. Once the bankside vegetation has flourished, the better fishing is likely to come on the tops of the gravel bars as both food and temperature will confine the carp there for at least some period of the day or night.

Initially on such new gravel pits the carp will only come to the surface in the hours of low light or at night. This is because there is no bankside vegetation for them to lie under. It has been said that carp like to lie in the shade of bushes. I am not at all sure they are trying to keep out of the sun, rather I think the bush gives them something snaggy to dive into should danger arrive close by. However, I know for a fact that carp, especially big carp, will lie motionless for a long time amongst the most awful tangle of roots and branches. They usually do this on the hard fished pit systems, where angler activity and therefore danger is at its greatest. It does mean though, that on an established pit with new bankside cover there is a good chance of getting a carp to feed on floating baits; certainly the most exciting way of all to catch them.

The wild carp has a long, sloping head and raised back which should distinguish it from a fast-growing common carp, which may have a hump back, but will have a small head.

Go Fishing for Carp

Corners of the lake, channels or bays are also affected by wind direction. This pushes any surface-borne debris into a confined area and it doesn't take long for the carp to get in there and mop it all up. Often the debris will look like a scum in a corner, and I advise a very careful approach as the fish are likely to be just under the surface. Far better to sit back quietly and fire out a few floating baits, not into the corner of the bay, but upwind so they drift down quietly . . . and just watch. If the fish feed first time, count yourself lucky. More likely you will see a "hump" rocking the surface as a carp comes to investigate. If spooked it may boil away angrily, without ever sucking the bait into its mouth, although to the untrained eye it looks as though it was taken. If this happens to me, despite the fact that I am probably on a knife edge, I never move the bait. To do so would confirm the carp's suspicions, so I let it drift right into the rubbish in the corner of the bay and leave it for five minutes. If the carp is spooked he will be long gone anyway, if he isn't he may come back and take. With floater fishing, never be in a rush to move.

This same principle applies to the level bottomed standard club water where overhanging trees create snags, and there are secluded bays. Don't worry if some of the bays are only a couple of feet deep. If the carp want a good feed they won't hesitate to work around in there. Another place to look in the old estate lakes is the inflow and outflow drainage ditches. After heavy rain, provided it has come with a warm westerly airflow, the draw off at the lake outflow will concentrate any floating insects or other food particles. The same goes for the inflow. In hot weather especially, the increase in oxygen, coupled with the food items washed in by the rainfall will be an inducement to any carp. For some reason I find the outflows fish best at night, while the inflows fish best at dawn! I have still to fathom this out, but I suggest you try it a few times before discounting it.

Other hotspots include those that are man made. On flat bottomed lakes, where there is little in the way of weedbeds, sunken branches or overhanging trees to create some sort of holding area for the carp, angler baits will do it for you. On heavily fished waters the bait always gets put in the same place every day and night for at least the first four months of the season. The time to fish these is when locals have dismissed the swim as "dead", and moved off to bait another. Leave it for a couple of days, then bait very lightly in the same spot, as the carp will still be returning there to see what is left. They may just pick up a few loose offerings before they become too suspicious.

Canals

As for other places, canals must come second place to larger stillwaters. They always make quaint fishing pictures, but I have never had a great deal of faith in extracting either a very big carp, or a bag of carp from a canal. It seems too narrow for my liking. I have had fish from them though, and they are well worth looking at, though you have to appreciate that much of the canal will be

Most still waters and canals have carp in them, and they travel throughout most of the water system. They can be caught at the surface or on the bottom, out in the centre of a lake, or within inches of the margins.

devoid of any fish. They are going to be found in hotspots, and for this reason I suggest the opposite bank from any towpath is the best place to look — especially if there is a "flash", or open area excavated to allow the old barges to turn around. Here it may be a little deeper, and provided there isn't too much boat traffic, carp will be in the far corner of the flash.

This is classical floater territory: some canals are clear, and being narrow, will put you close to the fish. Heavy bolt rigs and lead systems are unlikely to bear fruit here; instead, you should surface or at least floatfish for them. Almost any area where the bankside vegetation has grown over a bit is the place to look. So too are any beds of lily, or what I call arrowleaf. The carp may well be foraging on the leaves, looking for snails. Polarising glasses and a long peaked cap are the required items for fish spotting. Canals fish well for either a single fish, or several by prebaiting in the evening and coming back at dawn. The main drawback I have found is that no matter how carefully you play a carp, the commotion in such a confined area is likely to spook any others that may be around.

The best way to locate carp on a canal you either don't have first hand knowledge of, or which has no known or visible holding areas, is to select what you feel to be a suitable half-mile stretch, walk quietly along it, and scatter floating baits along its whole length. In the early evening you can do this using a cheap floater like sugar puffs or flavoured Chum mixer dog biscuits. Then, go for a pint and walk back along the stretch looking for visible signs of floating baits and carp.

Using this technique, on more than one occasion while I have been playing out a carp to the net, I have seen out of the corner of my eye some dimples on the surface two hundred yards away, against the sunlight, unhooked the fish, walked down, and hooked the other within fifteen minutes! It surely doesn't happen all the time, just enough to make it worth mentioning.

I have also heard anglers suggest you lay a line of loose feed for, say two hundred yards along the centre of the canal, culminating in a heavily baited area. This is intended to draw the carp from afar to the baited patch. However, supposing a carp comes across the bait halfway down the line, and starts eating his way along it . . . in the

OPPOSITE direction to the main baited patch! There must be a 50% chance of that happening surely? That some very big carp live in some of Britain's canal waterways I do not dispute, but I never feel they are capable of sustaining huge catches of low to middle double-figure fish. As another venue from which to take this species, however they should certainly be added to your list.

Fast-Flowing Rivers

The carp is not a lover of boiling, surging river torrents, yet in a few places on the continent, they are known to lie in fast water below rapids. I cannot believe they do too much feeding here; possibly they are there to clean themselves after spawning. The oxygen content in such turgid water is very high, and may help them recover faster. I would think the chances of contacting a very big carp under such conditions are rare indeed. Any big fish will need a constant supply of rich feed, which it would not be able to find in fast, turbulent water as it is whisked away too quickly. It would also burn up a lot of muscle tissue and energy simply fighting the fast current just to stay in the position where the most food is going to pass it.

I fished for some river carp with Bruce Vaughan on a fast Pennsylvania river, and those fish were as cagey as I have ever known. The truth is we couldn't get them to take, and although not large fish they proved very wary. We also found double-figure carp on the Juniata river in the same state. We were actually after Muskellunge and smallmouth bass. When I spotted the vast shoals of carp they proved ultra-spooky to get to in only two feet of water, and in fact hid their heads in the weedbeds, with the rest of their body clearly visible. I suppose they felt safe, like a child with a blanket over its head. We could easily have netted those fish out, without even resorting to rod and line.

Slack Water and Slow-Moving Rivers

Possibly the only place you may get a big carp is in slack water near lock gates, or in the slack of a weirpool. I have seen carp to around

15 lb on the Hampshire Avon when I have been after barbel — but they were tucked in behind weedbeds to keep out of the main flow. One of the problems with approaching fast-water carp is that you cannot sit on a swim with the reel bale arm open as you can on a stillwater; the current keeps pulling coils of line from the reel. You must either fish with a bolt-rig technique whereby the fish hooks himself, or touch ledger by holding the rod and feeling for the bite.

An easier proposition is a slow-moving river. Certainly there are some carp to 30 lb in many of our bigger, slow rivers like the Thames. I remember as a youngster spotting some above Pangbourne at a roadside layby. I was heavily into bleak at the time, and to see "monsters" of possibly 5 – 8 lb swimming around in front of me started my hands shaking. Anywhere the river widens and the pace of the current slows, is where the carp should be. The slowing of the current allows the bottom to become littered with debris, and silt from any floods can build up; an ideal place to find the bloodworm larvae. If the water slows and shallows, this same sedimentation allows lilies to grow. These give shade to the carp (and food in the shape of snails), so look there as well. Remember also that much of the Thames has lush banksides with overhanging trees. Many of the chub swims I fish have willows or other branches trailing in the water, and where this occurs on a far bank, you will find carp.

You need to approach by boat, position yourself upstream and drift floating baits down to the swim. Better still, if you can get permission, step out on the bank and get closer to the swim, but not so close as to spook the fish. The carp on a far bank are more likely to be in a feeding mood than those on the footpath side, where bankside activity is at its greatest. They will be well used to the wash from houseboats and cruisers, so don't let that bother you too much. If you can only get to the swim by boat, moor it broadside to the current with a weight at each end to secure it. That should stop it swinging about in the current, which makes for difficult bite registration.

On my own nine-foot glass boat I put out a roll of rubber-backed carpet to deaden the sound of anything I might drop like a shot box or flask. I also used to put a square of carpet on the bow and stern

Habitat

Carp have an extendable mouth for rooting in soft mud on the bottom. Soft paste baits can still be home-made for those who enjoy fishing with them.

so when I lifted the concrete weights over, they wouldn't make any grinding noises to put the fish off. Another tip is to drill a couple of holes in the gunnels to take miniature banksticks for supporting the rods.

A better place to look is in the back edge of the current from old locks and side cuttings. The water here is much slower, except when the locks open, and that sudden surge of water will churn up any bloodworm and food items on the bottom. When the boat goes through and that water starts to settle, the carp, and other fish, will have an easy feed without having to root around on the bottom. The lock areas can also respond well to big baits, but groundbaiting

43

in an isolated area is not so successful for the reason stated i.e. the bottom gets churned up as the lock gates open.

A good time to try baiting is after the last boat has gone through in late evening. Then the carp will move on to a groundbaited patch. Or if (as many places ban night fishing) you cannot stay late, you can do even better by baiting up after the last boat has passed through, then return at dawn and get in three or four hours' fishing before the boats start moving downriver again. You can always ask the lock keeper what time he thinks the last boat should come through.

In the larger weirpools you may find difficulty due to the depth of water. I have seen good carp cruising in the slack water right at the edge of the main torrent of river. Remember that in low water conditions the lock keeper is likely to have several sluices closed and these will be highly oxygenated, but almost still; an ideal place to look for carp. You will probably be unable to fish from the weir sills or sluice edges, so approach it with the boat. Use either floating or slow sinking baits, and watch the bow in the line where it enters the water for signs of a bite. Chances are good that you might also sort out some pretty hefty chub using this technique.

Because the carp has a liking for slow moving or still water, you must not neglect even the tiniest farm pond. Years ago someone might have introduced a few fingerling carp to keep down the mosquito population, but those fingerlings quietly pack on weight until the water can push them no further in weight. The ceiling for that weight depends on the depth of the pond and amount of food available. It may be two pounds, or it may be ten pounds. But the chances are good that those fish will respond very favourably to the most basic rigs and baits, at least for the first few times of capture.

Weather and Temperature

That the differing weather conditions we get in the British Isles affects fish behaviour, is well known to anglers. Temperature change coupled with wind direction are in my experience the two most important factors. As described previously, the prevailing wind in our country is south-westerly, but in fact any wind that pushes food into a corner of the lake for several days in a row will draw the fish. Anglers think that night is always the best time for carp because they normally feed then. This is not always the case, as carp will feed whenever they feel the urge. Having said that though, they are more likely to feel settled enough to search close to your bank at night, simply because the amount of angler activity has been reduced by then.

Carp do not possess an amazingly high IQ. That they learn is what makes them a difficult adversary, but they do not have the power to reason. They learn from association, in much the same way as pets are taught tricks by offerings of food. When your pekinese gets up from his bed, takes a six pack out of the fridge, and punches in the movie channel on your TV is the time you should start to worry. If you use the same techniques and baits as other anglers, then over a period of time those carp will come to ASSOCIATE that bait with a trip to the landing net. If you give them something different they are more likely to take it. They must have some sort of memory retention, but it can only be limited, and for a limited period of time.

In this way they associate certain weather conditions with being good times to feed. I hold a theory that the insect life below the surface is affected by barometric pressure changes. Insects being the main food, barometric pressure therefore directly affects the carp. So when you think they feed best in low pressure weather systems, it may be it is just because of the profusion of insect activity around them. Years ago it was thought the carp lay dormant in the mud all winter and did not feed. We now know this to be untrue thanks to those legions of carp anglers who spent many uncomfortable hours during the winter months to prove they could be caught. Temperature change does of course affect them, but only because the insect food chain is at its weakest in very cold weather.

To conserve energy, the carp in winter, feed for shorter periods, maybe only once in the day or night. In the warmer summer months they can feed right through the day, even in bright sunlight, contrary to the popular opinion that they go to sleep until nightfall! Their blood temperature changes with the surrounding water temperature, which in turn affects their metabolic rate. They do everything much slower in cold water. If there is an optimum temperature range to try carp fishing I would put it between 55 degrees and 65 degrees Fahrenheit. In cold weather the oxygen content of the water is higher so the fish can survive in a "static" state i.e. lying still in the water with their gills barely moving. In summer the surrounding water temperature rises, their blood temperature goes up, their metabolic rate increases, but the oxygen content will be lower. The fish will need to feed more because its respiratory system is more in use, and energy is consumed quicker. This is why you sometimes get fish kills in low water, high-temperature summer conditions. The oxygen level drops below a level that can sustain the fish.

Should the water become excessively hot, the fish will stop feeding entirely, and will be more intent on staying alive by maintaining a good oxygen flow over its gills. No, I don't know what that critical temperature is, otherwise I could save myself a lot of fishless days! Doubtless somebody could come up with an oxygen testing device that could be cast out into the swim, to see if it was worth fishing. Alternatively, you could cast around the lake until you found somewhere where the oxygen level was higher. Maybe near an inflow stream, in a windward bar, or in deep water. You could safely surmise that the shallows are not worth fishing in hot conditions due to low oxygen levels, and we know warm shallow water produces weed growth. However, the oxygen content of a water is not affected entirely by temperature alone. These same plants give off oxygen during the daylight hours, so there must be a balance between warm temperatures and shallow water that deplete oxygen and therefore reduce carp feeding times, and shallow water that is warm, but may have an added oxygen "boost" through increased weed growth.

The real problem as far as the carp is concerned is when that same weed dies off, and the decaying matter takes out more oxygen from the water than the green plants are putting in. This can, in extreme cases, completely de-oxygenate a water sufficiently to start a fish kill. It was also thought at one time that a fully scaled carp variety like the common carp might have a better body insulation that the less scaled mirror carp or the scaleless leathers. I don't feel this theory to be too solid, otherwise the first of the carp varieties to die because of warm water temperatures would all be commons, as they would be the first to "overheat". An interesting theory though.

In deep water there occurs a stratification of water layers in which the temperature ranges are clearly felt. Warm water rises to the surface, cold sinks deeper, where the two meet is called the thermocline, and on a large body of water the wind direction can actually tilt the warmer water into the windward end of a lake. This only occurs on waters deeper than about 30 feet, and as most carp waters in Britain are shallower than 30 feet, it possibly is not worth considering. All it does is to reinforce that you should fish into the wind, which of course as we know from the wind drift factor mentioned earlier, is where the carp are likely to be anyway.

In summer, when we get clear nights, the water will cool down in the shallows fairly rapidly, by radiation. In contrast, the area of shallow water that first receives the sunlight at dawn is going to be the area that warms up quickest. The land around the lake will hold some heat from daytime temperatures, especially if the ground rises several feet up. If the water is about two feet or less for some distance from the bankside, the landmass should let it cool down more slowly at night, than say, the centre of the lake. All these points are individually of minimal importance, but put together, they can make carp fishing a little easier and a little more successful.

Overcast nights after daytime sun are ideal for keeping the temperature stable, and this is a good time to try night fishing. Of all the 20-lb carp I have taken, not one came between the hours of 11 pm and 5 pm. On many waters there seems to be a "dead" period from about 12.30 pm to 3 pm, and while fish are taken between those hours I believe they are not the best.

The carp will feed whenever the fancy takes them, not necessarily because it is dark. They certainly have their regular patrolling routes, and I stumbled on some during an evening's tench fishing. It was on a stretch of a lake that was often used by match anglers for practice fishing, or by pleasure anglers just after anything. They had no chance of getting a decent swim as the carp anglers occupied all the popular areas on a virtual week-long basis. Match anglers and pleasure anglers invariably like to get home for tea by 6 pm, when they pack up and throw their leftover bait in. I work and so cannot really get to a water much before 6.30 pm. Bearing in mind the carp anglers were always on the water, I was surprised they hadn't realised the carp would learn of this free food and move in to mop it up. The food was also a different size, shape and colour than the regular "secret" carp baits, which gave the carp even more confidence in using it.

I lost of couple of fish straight away, that certainly were not tench. So each time I arrived I checked the ground in front of me, and the water's edge to see what the anglers had thrown in. If they were just packing up I would ask them. The first fish I took in this way weighed over 17 lb, and was landed on 4-lb line and a tench rod. There followed a season of several double-figure fish, and a couple of twenties. All this rattled the cage of the local carp boys who were ensconced in the swims for days on end with their special carp baits.

On another occasion I got similar results at another carp water by

Weather and Temperature

The author looks surprised with this big double-figure carp. He was half asleep when the rod started to disappear into the lake, and he just managed to grab the butt.

fishing after a match had been held, and took carp on a paste made from groundbait . . . as simple as that. Often the secret to successful carp fishing is to find a fish that is feeding first, and try it with one of the basic baits and rigs. Chances are good that you will make a connection.

The worst conditions I have ever found for carp are on still, clear nights with a full moon. Possibly the carp may be able to detect danger easier by moonlight I don't know, but other than the odd fish or two, I cannot recall too much success. Heavy cloud during the full moon period is fine, but a clear sky with a bright hard moon rising just makes me want to pack up and go home. The only time I find the moon an advantage is in the winter months when you get a mild spell, and have a carp feeding on floating baits close in. Then being able to see them actually take your floater down enables you to strike accordingly, without waiting for the bite to register on the alarm.

That carp will feed in the coldest of weather has already been proven, even when snow has covered the ground. The carp can be in spanking condition with a body sheen that glows with health and fitness. They also scrap very hard, and in my mind are in the best fighting condition you are ever going to find them in. From late autumn to early winter you will find them in the peak of condition, and they should still be putting on weight right up to the end of December. Then, if the winter is harsh, and the lakes ice over, they become dormant and use that body fat for insulation, thus losing a bit of weight. In winter it is particularly important to keep an eye on the weather. Any warm front moving in from the west or south-west is worth watching. There might be a full gale, so fish when the worst of the wind has abated. The back end of the coarse fishing season around the first two weeks of March can be particularly good if these warm winds bring a bit of rain. There have been some tremendous bags of fish landed during this two week period, but if we get a late winter, it doesn't fish quite the same.

If there is a sharp drop in water temperature they will go off the feed altogether, and even if the weather turns mild in winter, it will take a couple of days for the water to show signs of a rise. Sharp rises or falls are the worst periods to fish, while an even steady temperature, even if cold, is what you want to stand a chance of finding feeding fish.

Behaviour

There are several different ways to spot carp. The easiest is visually, in clear water, using polarising sunglasses and a wide peak hat to cut out the surface glare. This is also about the most difficult time to tackle carp. In clear water if you can see them, they can see you, plus all the knots, swivels and links on your end rig. Better to approach a clear-water carp with a freeline where nothing except the hookbait is on the line. Floating baits are also good in such conditions. You can learn a lot from watching carp, including the various ways they have of indicating their presence to you.

Humping

A quaint little term applied to a carp lying beneath a weedbed. The fish may be feeding on snails or shrimps, or could just be hiding. Whatever the reason, when they move, the weed over their backs rocks into a "hump". Spook a fish in a weedbed and you get an incredible "hump" followed by a carp barging its way through the weed in panic! I have actually caught carp when they are doing this. You may not see the whole fish outline, but you may see enough to judge which way he is pointed. Swing out a piece of floating crust, or a couple of Chum mixer biscuits about two feet in front of him, and watch his response. Often they lie still, twitch their fins a couple of times and swim up to engulf the lot, sucking in weed and all. Another time I have had to "dap" a piece of crust literally over their nose to attract their attention. If there are gaps in the weed and a small pocket of clear water in front of the fish, drop a piece of flake into it, then watch the line where it enters the water. Even if you can see the bait, don't strike until you see the line pull away, otherwise you will miss the fish, or just prick it.

Jumpers

No, not the woolly ones. Leaping carp are something that sets the pulse racing of most anglers new to carping. I was no different. When the Surrey Carp water of Cutt Mill had big lily beds in it (yes, I remember it well), I would sit in the rushes swim just starting to doze, when either a vixen fox screamed, an owl flew straight for me at head level, or a carp leapt out. The latter would leave a widening circle of ripples that rocked the lilies and kept me hovering over the old Heron indicators. Nothing happened of course, and nobody seems to know why they start leaping about all over the place. It has been said they do it to dislodge bloodworm on the bottom which they then feed on, but I think not. Having fished billfish around the oceans of the world and landed a few more than 70, I have come across this same spectacle. See a 70-lb sailfish leaping and you nearly need a change of shorts! Yet I have never had a strike from the fish in that area. I have heard a few skippers say they were catchable, but believe me I have pulled baits and lures through a few miles of water, and I've yet to slap the iron in one! I have caught sail from other areas on the same day and seen parasites and lice on them. I can only assume they are trying to dislodge them because they cause them discomfort. To explain leaping carp, my only theory is that leeches are the problem. The carp may have been hooked earlier and gone all sulky lying still on the bottom. The leeches attach themselves near the gills or vent, and thus cause them discomfort. Only my own personal theory, but it holds as much water as the next guy's! I would personally feel there is little chance of a carp taking your bait if it is a "jumper". But always try a cast as there may be other carp swimming near it and they might be in a mood to feed.

Behaviour

Bubblers

Almost anyone who has stood near water long enough will have seen bubbles popping up to the surface. I used to read all the old Mr Crabtree books as a youngster and never did know what caused fish to bubble. I know pike bubble to release gases they have taken in after striking at fish on the surface. I was recently told on good authority that perch are responsible for bubbles.

Both tench and carp are the main bubblers. Tench are easily recognised by its mass of pin-like bubbles that rise to the surface en-masse like a soapy foam, and stay there for some time before dispersing. Carp bubbles on the other hand are individually larger, but smaller in area. Bream also bubble, but as they would most likely be in a shoal those bubbles will be spread over a wide area. If

Nearly a twenty! Handle big carp carefully. They represent an investment to any club water and would be expensive to replace.

using a particle saturation bait like sweetcorn, when you see a shoal of bream over your baited patch, hit into even one of them and you can be sure you aren't going to get much sleep that night. What you should look for is a stream of two or three different bubbles, even one, but it should be moving. If you use a swim marker, line up the bubbles as a guide and see if they are moving. If they continue coming up in the same place the chances are good that it won't be a fish at all, but just natural gases escaping from the decaying matter in the mud on the lake bed. If they move, and it's over or towards your baited area just sit and wait. If you recast you run the risk of spooking the fish entirely. If it is moving away from your area you have nothing to lose and everything to gain.

Depending on the depth of water you should aim to put your bait several feet in front of the line of bubbles. In shallow water of three feet or so, you should drop it ten feet away from the fish. Better still, overcast the bubbles and wind back quietly under the surface until you judge the distance from the fish. The fish may be entirely engrossed in snuffling about with its snout stuck into some delicious bloodworm about five inches down. That being the case he will probably not see the bait at all. You may get a line bite as the fish roots around, there is no way of knowing.

Mudding

This is a term I picked up from by bonefishing experience. As a fish roots around on the bottom, its fins stir up the silt on the lakebed and swirls it high up over its back. If in water of three feet or less the clouds of mud mushrooming around, and the occasional flash of a tail fin as the fish feeds feverishly are very noticeable. In deeper water rooting fish may colour water up to ten feet deep and indicate their presence with a borderline where the coloured water meets clear.

Once the initial mudding has subsided the suspended particles will still hang high in the water and if there is a below-surface current drift on a windy day be spread over a much wider area than the fish were feeding in. It also means that they might have finished feeding altogether even though the water is still coloured. This was a problem with bonefish in the Caribbean from Little Cayman island. The bonefish were in an enormous school. Spot them as soon as they started feeding and you could see which direction they were taking and work into an intercept position, but if the cloud got too big, you had no idea where to cast. What I tried to do then was judge which way the current, if any, was moving, go to the upcurrent end, then move down about one third into the mudded area.

The same technique can be applied to carp fishing. If the muddy area looks large and dispersed, move to the upwind end and where it starts from the clear water, and move down about one third. It's only a tip, but one of those extra tips that may put a fish on the bank for you!

There will be times when a shoal of small carp moving along, sends up the same clouds of mushrooming mud as a shoal of bream. The carp are fairly social fish, and the larger the shoal the smaller the size of fish. A shoal of big carp may consist of several double-figure fish and a couple of twenty pounders. In contrast a shoal of smaller carp might number thirty fish, but the top weight may only be four or five pounds. The more carp in a shoal, the more competitive they are likely to be, and the better bite you are likely to get. The bigger carp, those into double figures, are likely to stay together when resting, browsing or feeding together. The odd single fish may break away from the others to feed for a short period on its own, but it should return at some time during the same night or day. I liken this behaviour to that of the elephants in Africa who feed together, obviously have some social order, and when they get to a larger size possibly stay together most of their lives.

Boiling

This is a term I use for pinpointing exactly where a fish has moved. If you notice when a carp, or better still a tench nears the net, the water boils on the surface as their tail fin tries to drive them down to the bottom. When hooked far out they seldom do this as the angle of pull from the rod top is lower. As the fish nears the net though, the rod top will be trying to lift the fish vertically, and then their natural reaction is to pull away from it. That means the tail fin is towards you, and boils the surface in a big swirl. Tench do it all the time.

If you see this boil on the surface in shallow water, it may be due to a fish standing on its head to pick up a single morsel lying on the lake bed. It's a head down, tail up situation, and the tail action boils the surface. Occasionally you will see this when drifting out some floaters on a large lake, where the carp are well aware there may be a hook in one. If very nervous they will drift up to the bait, open their mouth but churn away quickly in fright, leaving a boil on the surface. It is at least an indication of carp on the surface, but I have seen them doing this in very windy weather when individual fish spotting is particularly difficult.

When fishing for 100-lb tarpon in the Florida Keys in very shallow water, the same observation was used to locate this huge fish. They can roll on the surface to take in air, or be spotted visually. Yet when windy conditions ripple up the surface you have to look for "funny water" as the guides call it, indicating the fish's presence near the surface. The same goes for carp. Even when there is a hefty ripple on the lake or gravel pit you can, by watching the surface, spot this area of disturbed water indicating carp movements. Basically anything that interrupts the regular wave pattern causing a flat spot, or counter ripple can be caused by carp. There are occasions when other species do the same. A pike taking a rudd near the surface will disturb the surface. Tench, if the spawning season is late due to a cold spring can also cause it. A shoal of bream rolling over a baited area can cause the same disturbance. All I can suggest is that you treat all movements as potential signs of carp, and fish accordingly.

Bow-Waving

Some anglers have different views on a carp bow-waving. Some feel they only do this when alarmed in shallow water, making an arrowhead shape on the surface as they rush along. But I have observed it in deep water, though I would agree that spooked fish are the most likely cause. Casting a floating bait to a fish that is travelling quickly like this will rarely be taken. In fact I have seen them kick down a gear and go ever faster! Fast bow-wavers, even in shallow water are still a means of locating carp. Even if they are feeding naturally in shallow water they can spook just because the very depth makes them nervous. This could be due to herons taking a stab at them at dawn or dusk. I think it is an instinctive nervousness, and have watched them spook on the other side of a lake where nobody could have spooked them. Even a seagull flying over the water can spook carp, or a mallard landing close by.

I would advise watching for two things. Keep an eye on the bow-waving fish and see where the disturbance tails off. Sometimes that fish will slow from a sprint to a cruise, then stop. Rest it a couple of minutes, then cast a floating bait, if possible, about thirty feet in front where the bow-wave stops. Most of the time you don't get a take anyway, but it has worked just enough times to make it worth giving it a shot for ten or fifteen minutes.

The other point is to look for fish moving, or cruising, very slowly just under the surface. Occasionally their dorsal will show. I have no idea why they cruise at this level, and I feel sure they are not looking for food. They are however an excellent possibility for taking a floating bait. Either scatter some loose floaters in front of the direction you estimate they are going, or go straight to it, and drop a floater right at them. The latter has been very successful for me; put the floater just far enough in front to avoid spooking them. A heart-stopping method of fishing, I always feel the pulse race a bit when that floater kisses the surface in front of them!

Circlers

The first time I came across carp circling was in Greece, on the Halkidiki peninsula. I heard from a charter boat captain that there were carp in a pond on a golf course adjacent to the hotel complex. I had already been mullet fishing with some success in the harbour, using dinky little spin outfits and 4-lb line. I wasn't equipped for carp fishing and had to make do with bread. I hadn't made provision for the five thousand fishes though! Dodging golf balls I looked at the two lakes which were pea green and very, very unfishy. I saw what I thought was a clump of brown algae in the centre of one lake, and suddenly realised it wasn't drifting down at the same pace as the surface ripple. See what I mean about noticing something different about regular ripple pattern disturbance? As I crept closer I saw that the clump of brown algae was in fact a dozen or more carp, all huddled round in a circle, mouths gulping at the surface. At first I thought they were all feeding on something, but it quickly became apparent they were not. In the other lake, carp were doing the same, all swimming in a perfect circle, all gulping away at something. Whether this was some bizarre social behaviour akin to animals in a zoo pacing up and down in cages too small for them — perhaps the pond was too small for the volume of fish — I don't know, but I interrupted them with a piece of floating crust. Far from spooking them I hit a fish, only about 5 lb, but a good scrap on the bonefish rod. To cut a long story short, I returned next day with a friend, and between golf balls hammered out something over 120 lb of carp before we were removed for fishing what turned out to be a millionaire's ornamental pond! We were lucky we weren't slung in some Greek jail. Later that year I read in one of the fishing monthlies than another angler had seen exactly the same thing happening in a British water. The Letters Page remained unusually dormant, so I assume we were either the only anglers in the world to see such an occurrence, or nobody knows why the carp do this "circling" behaviour. The moral of this is if you ever see them doing it, get a floating bait in there in double quick time, as they definitely will express some sort of interest in it!

Margin Cruisers

The carp that works along the edge of a lake is termed a margin fish. On a hard fished water they may only move in close during the hours of darkness. On some lakes, especially gravel pits where anglers are constantly bombarding the gravel bars and shelves with two ounce leads, the carp will come in close. On day-ticket waters where no night fishing is allowed, very big carp will move in close to the bank to mop up any leftover baits thrown in by the angler who has to be off the water at dusk. Likewise after matches or after holiday family anglers who tend to leave at dusk. If you can move

Behaviour

The author with a big double-figure mirror carp taken by margin fishing at night. Big carp will often feed close to the bank after dark, so keep your movements to a minimum.

in to the same swim and fish the last couple of hours before closing, there is every chance you can pick up a margin fish.

It may always be worth throwing a few loose samples near the margins, and fish one rod there, the other out in the traditional area. Often the margins fish better. Just how close carp will move in was illustrated to me when fishing a lake known for its head of small carp. Most were around five pounds, and a double was an unusual bonus; however I could be sure of hitting a few fish during an evening session. I was using soft paste baits which I had to keep re-kneading to make them pliable. They were sticky, and I got covered with gunky colouring and flavouring. Every hour I used to wash my hands in the side of the lake, right by the rods. The first couple of times, I noticed line bites on the indicators as I bent to wash my hands. Fish were obviously close and my movement had scared them. Later in the session when I washed my hands, two or three carp bolted away, right under the bank. Those carp had come in under the rods to pick up the leftovers I had washed from my hands! One night I was washing the excess off very quietly when a 5-lb carp eased up and actually nipped my finger. I jumped back with shock and saw several others bolt away.

It took me about five minutes to put a bait in there and sometimes I just lowered it in from the rod top. Yet those carp were the very devil to hit. Either I missed them completely or they bolted away so hard they hooked themselves. Once I even had a rod towed in, but the blank floated and I cast out a pike plug to retrieve both rod, and the carp! From that point on many locals started to floatfish luncheon meat about two feet from the bankside and overhanging bushes with some considerable success.

Margin patrollers also respond very favourably to floating baits, best used when there is a very slight surface drift into a bay. There may be a natural surface scum there, and the carp are likely to visit the area anyway. The main point to remember about margin fishing is that the fish are likely to be very easily spooked, and therefore you need patience and care. This sort of fishing is best suited to floating baits, or very slow sinkers. Forget the use of leads and bolt rigs. You need a delicate approach to get the most from one of the more exciting methods of taking carp.

Reed Knockers

Any fish that moves through a reed margin or lily bed will knock a few of the stems. Any movement against lilies is particularly noticeable as the whole leaf on the surface will twitch as a fish bumps through. Reed stems are close together, and may only be in a foot or so of water, but big carp will still move through them. They may be sucking shrimps or snails from the stems or underside of the leaves, but at least you will know they are there. Also other species have a habit of feeding the same reed beds as the carp. They can be rudd or roach but they are more likely to be knocking away at one particular stem to dislodge food.

The carp on the other hand will move bodily through the reeds so that one or more stems will knock in unison, so the direction of the fish's progress may be seen by watching the stems. The unfortunate point is that big tench will do the same, and they could be the size of a small carp. They also push through lily beds, but as I said previously, treat all movements as coming from a carp and sooner or later you will hit a fish. This is again floater territory, and care should be used in dropping a bait to them. The eighteen inches of water in a reed bed will be clear so the fish can see the line, or be disturbed by the cast. In lily beds you do at least have the option of dropping your bait quietly on top of the weed then tweaking it quietly off. In really thick Canadian Pond weed that has bloomed up on the surface, you may find the bait has to be dropped noisily with a plop to actually attract the fish. This soft weed is unlikely to knock as a fish moves through it, but the art of spotting "weed-knockers" is all part of the experience of locating the fish in the first place. All these tips are useful. Learn them and half the battle is won.

Carp Control Measures

Most anglers will be aware that the transportation of fish from one water to another is illegal, without the proper documentation and approval from the relevant water authorities. The main reasoning behind this is to prevent, or at least minimise the spread of any disease from one water to another. This could be likened to a farm being quarantined due to an epidemic of Foot and Mouth disease. That is an extreme analogy, but fish diseases are capable of wiping out the entire stock of a lake. Many anglers do not really understand the importance of this, as the carp, and other species in our lakes and canals, are not used for human consumption. If they were, research would probably reveal any diseases at an early stage, and nip them in the bud. As it is, most of the diseases are reported by anglers who see either dying or dead fish in the margins of a lake when they go fishing.

The problem occurs when a fisherman wants to put his favourite species into another water that may not have any in it. He does it illegally, taking the fish at night, and without realising, jeopardises all the occupants of his favourite water, by introducing a fish that may be riddled with disease. That's mainly why the law of no fish transportation without water authority approval exists. The authority, should you approach them, will generally take a few samples of fish from a netting, and run various tests to ensure they are disease free. If they are shown to have a disease, they will refuse the paperwork to move them to another water, but the fish will be allowed to live in the water they are in at that time.

Carp Control Measures

As an illustration of what can happen with illegal fish movements, we only have to look back to the fishing scene when the controversial zander were introduced. There was a public outcry from many anglers that this species, not a native of British waters, would cause the destruction of many of our cyprinid species. As it happened, the zander, once stocked (initially done legally), thrived on a diet of roach, rudd and bream fry in the Fenland waters that became home for them. They thrived to such an extent that there was a boom in catches, and being a new species with a good growth rate, much publicity surrounded the capture of perpetual new British records. There developed a popular following with zander fishermen, who decided they wanted to catch even bigger zander from other waters. The zander suddenly appeared in dozens of different waterways, and soon spread through lake and canal systems. Numbers eventually levelled out however, when other anglers killed every zander they caught and stocks of their prime food fish became reduced.

As they became less numerous, the bigger fish became more valuable. Rumours on the angling grapevine said that zander were changing hands for money, rather than just for someone's sporting needs. Which all draws me back to the carp. As water becomes more at a premium than ever before and angler density increases, publicity over big carp catches increases, and soon the species has developed "legs" and started to be transported between waters. Anglers today want instant big fish, and cannot wait ten years for carp to grow to a good size, plus carp farms are also at a premium for supplying big fish. Night fishing for carp is very successful, but also the cloak of darkness allows many unsportsmanlike goings on to be enacted.

The carp can be kept for some time out of water. As long as they are kept moist, maybe in a wet hessian sack, they can be driven many miles and stocked into another water. As long as ten years ago many of us had a feeling this was going on, and today it is rife. A double-figure carp can change hands on the "black market" for several hundred pounds, and even a 20-lb carp, if in good condition and a fast grower, can make £500. This huge sum obviously attracts some anglers to steal fish either for their own waters, or to sell on to others. But now things may finally be starting to change as angling clubs have found a way to record all of their stock. For small angling clubs with a limited membership, the cost of buying in a carp legally may represent a large slice of their income. Some clubs even hold fund raising events to buy a few big carp. Then in one night a single angler steals the fish and breaks the heart of all those genuine fishermen. One of the large gravel pit complexes near my home is home to some jumbo carp. They don't get stolen too often but they are moved from one lake to another in an effort to hide their whereabouts from other anglers. Very unfair, and certainly selfish.

I spoke with John Levell, who runs the highly successful Somerley Fishery in Hampshire. John has decided to stamp out fish stealing once and for all by implementing his own photographic record of every single big carp in his fishery. Somerley is a superb

An angler admires a Broadlands carp. This venue is one of the most prolific in England available on a day ticket, and with a catch return of several hundred double-figure fish each season.

water, and can be fished through Ringwood & District AA. The carp in this rich gravel pit system are all grown on from the original stocking in October 1977. Those fish were put in at just eight ounces and have now been caught to nearly 30 lb! They are usually in perfect condition, and during the close season John feeds them on with high-protein trout pellets; they must be some of the finest carp in England.

It was in 1984 that John's carp first started disappearing. All carp have some distinguishing marks: scars from spawning damage, cuts etc. (Damaged fins are no good as an identification mark though because they regrow.) They are as individual as fingerprints and, if properly documented, can form an invaluable identification record for a fishery. As carp prices increase in line with fish stealing, so more clubs and private fisheries are implementing record keeping.

The first carp disappeared from Somerley in August 1984. John knew who had stolen it, and that it had gone to a syndicate water only thirty miles away, but there was no way he could prove anything until the fish was recaptured. Quietly his own anglers started questioning anglers who fished the syndicate water about their captures. All fisherman like to show off pictures of their catches, and finally they found the carp from Somerley in a fisherman's photo. John was notified and approached the owner who denied it was stolen. John showed him the photographic evidence and advised him that he would arrive at his lake, pump it dry, extract his carp then send the bill to the Estate that was leasing the water to the syndicate. This soon solved the problem, and the carp was returned at a weight of 24 lb having been stolen at 22 lb 10 oz. The system has worked, and now more clubs and fishery owners are protecting their stocks with photo-identification.

Many fisheries today have purchased carp from farms at large weights, and with the angling pressure for more and bigger carp I feel sure the 'farmed' carp will soon form the main part of most angler's catches. It is possible to draw comparisons with these stocked carp and the large trout stocked at our small stillwaters. There have been calls previously for a separate listing for both wild (naturally grown) and ex-farmed fish, but there is obviously a difficulty in differentiating them where the two co-exist in the one water. There is also a possibility that the British record could be broken by a carp artificially reared at a carp farm on the continent then flown in to be caught from some tiny syndicate water. What should be appreciated is not the fact that the next British record carp could be a farmed fish, but that farmed fish can provide entertaining fishing in a short space of time. They are here to stay and we should do our best to protect whatever stock is swimming in our clubs, or private fisheries.

Fish Retention and Photography

Many of you will undoubtedly want some sort of record of your catch, be it large or small. You are entitled to it, as carp fishing is not an easy game. When you spend a session measured in days and nights rather than hours and require some sort of record of the catch, you will need to keep them in good condition. Years ago carp were retained in keepnets. If the nets were knotless they did less damage to the fish's scales. But the problem with the dorsal fin on the carp, is that the leading ray, or spine on the dorsal can become ragged and catch in the mesh. It is the very devil to remove and you may even have to cut the mesh.

Nowadays most clubs have quite rightly banned the retention of carp of any size in keepnets. I do it occasionally, with permission, for articles, but it is far easier to weigh them, take a photo and return them, than it is to spend precious time in the laborious task of cutting dorsal spines from keepnets. Today the "sacking" method is employed, where the "sacks" are made from a special lightweight black material with large holes in it to allow a flow of oxygenated water through the fishes' gills. The old hessian sacks are tombs as the fish can suffocate through lack of oxygen. On some waters even the approved sacks are starting to be banned. One of the main problems, even with approved sacks, is that when the angler tethers his catch in an area of shallow water, where summer

Weigh slings are now custom made with the carp in mind. This one features a zip and closing cords for attaching to the scales. It can also be used as a retention sack if you wish to obtain photographs of your fish.

daytime temperatures can soar, the carp gets stressed, or worse still, expires completely. If you retain carp, make sure you put the sacked fish in the deepest water you can find, and in shade, not out in bright sunlight. The fish is in a black sack so the sunlight should not bother it, but remember black is the colour that absorbs heat readily. I feel a carp sack should be black on the inside, but white on the outside to reflect the heat.

The obvious answer to all this is to take photos of the fish as soon after weighing as possible. Today, compared with the outlay on carp equipment, the cost of a reasonable 35 mm camera is nominal. Practika, Zenith, Olympus, Canon and Minolta are all good. The camera body you are likely to buy will probably have a standard 50 mm lens with it. This is perfect for what you will be doing i.e. taking shots of angler plus fish. You can buy colour print film very cheaply, 100 ASA is the best film speed to get. You can go to 200 ASA for low light, but then you only need to purchase a flash and you can take your shots any time of the day or night. If you have a friend or another angler close by they will probably focus up and take the picture for you. If you fish alone, like I nearly

Fish Retention and Photography

This is a rare shot of the amazing leaping carp of Petersfield lake. Actually it was taken by the author using a tripod and self-timer that didn't work. Better to use a bulb air release which you can squeeze to release the camera shutters when you feel the fish is calm. This was taken in the author's early days when he believed everything should be camouflaged, including his umbrella — even at night!

always do, take a tripod and bulb air release along.

To take a picture of yourself all you do is set up the focus on something like your bedchair, allow a foot either side for the head and tail of your fish, or take along a wooden frame stick, putting it in the ground and focusing on it. Then, pick up the fish and move to the frame. Most cameras have an automatic shutter release, this can be used instead of the manual bulb air release. The only problem here is that the carp can leap out of your arms just as the automatic shutter fires, and you get a carp in mid air! With the bulb air release you can kneel on it the precise moment you feel the carp has settled. Every picture should be OK.

If you use black and white film you will find it both cheaper to buy, and also to get prints taken from the negatives. Pick a film with a fairly high ASA rating, somewhere around 400 ASA; this will allow you to take good pictures in low light conditions without the use of flash. Always remember to keep any light behind your back so the subject is well lit, but avoid your shadow falling into the picture. Best to take the shot at a slight angle, rather than face on. Today some carp anglers are using home videos to record any fish, but the few I have seen look like those American muscle shows. The guy lifts the carp out of the sack then poses around with it statically held in different positions. The object of a video is to record movement. Why not show baiting up, casting, hooking and netting a fish. Shots of wildlife, swims etc all make a more interesting record. Remember to fit a muffle on the microphone otherwise you get wind noise in the background.

You should fit a screw-on skylight or UV filter which will enhance both still and video photography. If you use still photography take several shots at different exposures just to make sure at least one frame comes out. For easy use I suggest using a fully automatic camera for stills photography. All the leading makes produce automatics now, most with built-in flash and focusing. All you do is point and press. They take all the 35 mm range of films, and the Minolta automatics are about the best. Pocket size, they give excellent pictures if standard procedures are followed, and are far easier than the manual range of cameras.

Techniques

Floatfishing

To the modern carp angler, the use of a float would seem almost quaint, yet this method can still be used to pick up an extra fish or two. If match fishermen still hit carp up to 30 lb when fishing the float and light lines, it cannot be said to be too quaint! Undoubtedly the best of the carp fishing as we know it today comes from a bait fished at either extremes: hard on the bottom, or floating on the surface. The mid-layers of water seem apparently sterile, but that may be because so few anglers fish a bait there. With shallow water, there is little need to use the float, except as a means of indicating a bite immediately a fish has picked up a bait. Correctly shotted, with just a quarter of an inch of float top showing, the angler has one of the most delicate bite indication devices available.

There are basically two situations where a float can be used. The first is on a water that has not been heavily fished by anglers, including carp fishermen fishing tight lines to bolt rigs, or match fishing. Either party will put carp on red alert, and they will be wary of any terminal tackle in the water. If unfished, or rarely fished, the carp will be more confident, and the float can be used. Although I have stressed that it is a means of getting a bite quickly, it is still a pleasurable way of fishing carp. Of course you can still take those carp on traditional bottom fishing techniques, but why waste the opportunity of floatfishing them first. Scare them with the float and you still have the option of bottom fishing. The same cannot be said of bottom fishing. Tight line bolt rigs undoubtedly make fish wary, and it is pointless floatfishing them afterwards.

If you have a feature to fish by such as marginal weed, lilies or overhanging branches, you need only a single stem waggler float, bulking the main shot under the float and leaving a single bb shot about a foot from the hook. Depending on the amount of surface drift, you may need to slightly overdepth the float, to allow for the shot to rest on the silt or mud and hopefully stop the bait dragging out of position. Carp have a tendency to refuse a drifting bait. For bait, carpet the area with boilies, bread, paste baits or whatever takes your fancy. But do not bait too heavily. You can get an indication of a carp in the swim either by bubbles, clouds of mud, or the float jolting as a feeding carp bumps into the line. Generally the response will be better the closer to any feature you can get. Let your main line strength correspond with any snags; somewhere over 8 lb should be about right. You can drag a carp out of soft weed but not out of a tangled web of fallen branches.

The other use for the float is in deep-water gravel pits. Both surface and bottom baits will catch, but divers, and of course anglers, have observed apparent disdain from carp swimming about in mid water. I put this down to the fact that most anglers are still thinking in terms of surface or bottom-fished baits. There is still that enormous area of water in between; the carp live there, so why not try to catch them from there? To do this you need to use a slow-sinking bait with almost neutral density, like breadflake that takes a long time to fall to the bottom, and therefore remains in the carp's "travel" zone longer. Boilies and paste baits are too heavy, and sink straight to the bottom, defeating the object of the exercise.

Some anglers have tried fishing a running ledger rig that allows a buoyant bait like crust to float up from the bottom. That's fine, but you get poor indication, and of course there is a huge angle of right-angled line to pick up on the strike, before you come tight to the fish, and set the hook. With free lining you have the ideal scenario of a slow sinking bait, but you have little indication of a take, other than a visual one. The answer is to use a float.

You need a bodied waggler this time as most gravel pits are open and susceptible to the breeze, which creates casting and drag problems. A light waggler prevents you from 'mending' the line to the float if it develops a belly in the surface ripple. A heavier bodied waggler, with the extra shotting, allows you to move the line without disturbing the float too much. All the shot should be bunched underneath the float, which allows just the weight of the bait to sink slowly through the depths.

Two points to remember when you cast. A big bodied waggler float may take two or three swan shots, so there is plenty of casting weight there. To avoid the whole rig falling in a crumpled heap you must cast hard, but feather the rim of the reel spool at the very last moment. If you do this correctly, and stop it just before it hits the surface, the float will stop first, allowing the bait to whip past and fall away from the float, and hopefully avoid any tangles. You also need to ensure the float stops and the bait travels past it to retain a straight line between the two for bite indication. If it all falls in a heap, a carp could take the bait then travel several feet before registering a bite. Those vital seconds allow it to spit the bait out if everything doesn't feel quite right. With a straight line between the two, any take registers on the float sooner. Of course a carp can still create slack between the bait and the float, but that is a chance you have to take. With all the weight under the float it will cock immediately, and it doesn't hurt to move it a foot or two towards you to tighten any slack if you think the bait did not fall away on the cast hard enough.

The best bait for this type of carping is breadflake. It absorbs water quickly and should sink at a slow rate. A bunch of lobworms can also work well. No fancy rigs, no special baits, just two of the best carp baits to use on a little fished water. Two more tips I can give you. If you want to fish a slower sinking bait, you can slow its sink rate by greasing the line from bait to float. Mucilin on the nylon does no harm and is generally used by trout fishermen who need to ensure their leader floats on the surface in order to present a dry fly. The tiny disadvantage this may have is that Mucilin on nylon makes it slightly opaque. This in turn may make it more visible to the fish. However, I imagine over the years that trout anglers have had the same problem, and they still catch trout using greased leaders.

Go Fishing for Carp

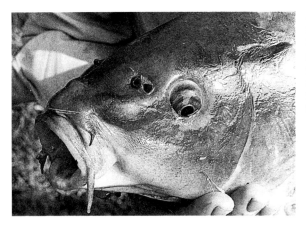

A perfect close-up of a carp, showing those four barbules in the corner, and on the top edge of the mouth. The large mouth indicates they are capable of taking very large baits.

In contrast, a bait that absorbs water very slowly and has trouble popping through the surface film, can be made to sink faster by degreasing the same length of line using either a commercially made degreasing pad, or some washing up liquid. I always carry a small bottle of diluted washing up liquid in my tackle box for just such an occasion. In fact you can treat the entire length of line if you want.

Having mentioned wagglers, which are my personal preference as they cast like bullets, you can also try floats like the Loafer, designed for chubbing. It too can take quite a bit of weight and still be shotted down to show just a quarter inch of tip. The advantage a waggler has is that you can take one shot off and leave it sticking several inches out of the water which is ideal when conditions are difficult, like in heavy rain or when there's a big ripple on a windy day. You can also find a problem with Loafers when the depth of water you are fishing exceeds the length of the rod tip to reel. Short of standing on your tackle box to cast with a deeper setting on your float (yes, I've done that too), it's best to use a sliding float. These can be purchased from your local tackle shop but make sure you get one that takes a couple of swan shot at the minimum. You can then fish at a predetermined depth by using a stop knot and bead. Remember the longer the sinking time, the more difficulty you will have in registering a bite, that is until the bait lies vertically beneath the float.

When you loose feed samples, however slow sinking they may be, they will always eventually land on the bottom. If the carp don't take them on the drop, it may be worth letting the float rest the bait just on the bottom. A suspended bait, while taken occasionally by carp, must look strange, and it is more likely to be taken either on the drop, or hard on the bottom.

One of the best places to fish a slow-sinking floatfished bait is alongside trees and other overhanging snags. Remember you don't have to use a shop-bought float. How about making up your own from small lengths of balsa wood painted either green or brown? You need only fish about three to six feet deep as the carp are likely to be near the upper layers of tangled branches. With small home-made "chips" of balsa you can afford to lose them in snaggy swims.

Floats can also be used for accurate casting into nooks and crannies in weeds on windy days. It is possible to use a specially-made controller float, but quite honestly any float taking a couple of swan shot will do. Controller floats such as these are ideally purpose made for floating bait fishing. Some incorporate a weight to make them cock, but they could hardly be described as giving the least resistance to a taking fish. They are best dealt with under the heading of "floating baits". However out of date, the humble float still has a place in the carp fisherman's armoury.

Bottom Fishing

This is a term I have only heard used in sea fishing circles, but it fits the world of carp so well I thought I would include it here. The carp, as we already have stated, is essentially a bottom-feeding species. That is why the mouth is extendable, the barbules located to sense taste and smell on the bottom. Its main diet, the blood-worm, is found in the soft silty mud on the bottom of the lakes. Although I have included a section on floating baits, which indicates they feed on the top as well, the majority of anglers consider bottom baits to be the primary method of catching carp.

The best rigs for bottom fishing are the simplest, most practical you can think of. Using a freeline, the only thing you need on the end is a hook. What could be more simple than that? The freeline is the way to minimise any resistance to a taking fish, because it has no snags; leads, beads, floats or booms to pull against. However, bite regulation is the drawback. Some anglers say that a bait lying on the lake bed when freelined has only a 50% chance of giving a decent bite registration. They take a 180 degree arc on the opposite side of the bait as being the area in which the fish can pull line away from you and thereby register a bite. But I know this to be untrue from my game fishing experience where I deal with large fish bellying line through the water.

When a fish moves virtually anywhere in a 360 degree arc, short of coming straight at you, a bite should register. Even when a fish moves towards you, if your indicator set-up is correct, it should register as a drop-back bite. What you have to do with freelining is maintain tight contact with the bait, and sit and watch your indicators for any sign of movement. On a hard fished water the practicalities of this are obviously limited, and it doesn't suit the angler who is used to going to sleep for long hours in the comfort of his bivvy. You also cannot really use light baits like seed baits, or particle baits when fishing at any sort of distance. The same principles of keeping tight to them for visual indication are important, but you simply cannot cast them. Add any weight and you are not freelining. With smaller seed baits and even boilies you should look to margin fishing where you only have a short distance to cast to a

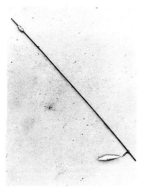 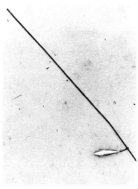 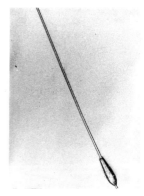

The Kevin Nash weighted anti-tangle tube for balanced rigs.

The Kevin Nash Anti-Tangle rig with soft tube.

The Kevin Nash Anti-Tangle rig with stiff tubing.

fish. Small seed baits like a couple of grains of sweetcorn sink slowly, and fished in conjunction with say, 10-lb line, they may not sink as the line tends to stick to the surface film. If this happens degrease with washing up liquid.

Freelining

For this reason, when freelining, I would use only large paste baits, which at least afford some decent casting weight. Years ago the par-boiled potato was all the rage. With a casting pad of crust in the bend of the hook, you could happily freeline a spud at sixty or seventy yards!

Larger paste baits are easier to handle, and in my mind are better. Use a big hook, a size 2 or larger, and keep the paste as soft as possible. If you mix it very stiff you are fishing with the equivalent of an oversized boilie. In contrast to some anglers, I mould the paste around the whole hook. I do not leave the point showing, as the bait will be soft and the hook drags through it on the strike. I like to fish my baits very soft, and then they are only suited to a gentle underhang swing out. If you need to cast any further than a couple or three rod lengths you have to put a small piece of twig or grass stem into the bend of the hook and then mould the paste around it. This stops it flying off on the cast.

Having mentioned that you need to keep close contact with a freelined bait, there are another two problems you are going to come up against. The first is that your bobbin weight may exceed that of the bait. This is obvious when you use, say, a washing up liquid bottle top in conjunction with two grains of sweetcorn. The problem is that the weight of the bobbin keeps pulling the bait back towards you. If the bobbin lies on the ground you don't get to see those all important drop back bites. Even a heavier paste bait, which weighs more than the bobbin when out of the water, may get pulled back if you haven't taken into account that anything in water weighs less than it does on land.

The answer is to use as light a bobbin as you can—heavy enough to take up the slack against the bait, yet not so heavy as to keep pulling back towards you. One of the best indicators can be made

Go Fishing for Carp

The author with a twenty pounder that fell to trout pellet paste made so soft it barely stayed on the hook. Using baits this soft, means you have to watch your bobbin indicators all the time.

by cutting up the coils of plastic spines on larger note books. You can then pinch on any additional weight in the shape of shot, until it counterbalances the weight of the bait in the water. I don't like to use monkey climb indicators anyway, and prefer a simple, short drop bobbin. Most of the time I will be sitting right next to the rods, hopefully not asleep, and will hit any bite before it reaches the butt ring.

The other drawback to using freelined bait is that some shallow waters suffer from sub-surface drift. Even a moderate breeze can put a current into the lake, and any belly in the line makes life difficult when you want to keep contact with the bait. A strong drift can also drag a bait out of position. In this situation there is a limit to when the freeline method can be used and if that is exceeded effectively, you should change to a ledger rig. The wind, if blowing across the lake from either side will put a belly in the line before you get chance to sink it. With a ledger rig you can tweak the line by the reel while keeping the rod top under water and sink the line without dragging the bait away from the baited swim. Freelining doesn't allow this, as any tweaking will drag the bait away. With a wind blowing straight in to your face it actually helps sink a line as the ripples break up the surface layer film. Try sinking a line on a glassy calm day and you will see what I mean. For this reason I always carry a small spray bottle of diluted detergent. Before I even thread the line through the rod rings I spray this mixture on the reel spool and know my first cast will have the line sinking straight away. Further applications can be applied when required. Simply wind the hook up into the tip ring so as much line as possible is on the spool.

Another problem some anglers have is when they try to tighten up too quickly after casting out. Sink the line first, then pull the bobbin down a couple of feet and leave it. The buoyancy of the line is greater than the bait so it will be sinking slower. Only when all the line has laid on the lake bed can you really tighten up and feel the weight of the paste bait. There is friction of a sort between the line and the lake bed, so use this to your advantage when tightening to the bait.

As to the bites, all should rise to the butt ring, but you may get a drop back bite as the carp moves towards you. Leave it for five seconds in case the fish has sucked in the bait, blown it out, and is simply lying behind it watching. Then turn the reel handle slowly, and gently pull the line in front of the bobbin until you feel the weight of the bait. If it won't tighten up at all, the chances are the bait has gone, a problem you get with paste baits that are soft. Many times I have started to draw line back to re-adjust the bobbin and felt a fish at the other end. At that very same instant that my mind has said "Oh God, there's a carp on the end . . . has he felt me and will he drop the bait?", while the carp at the other end has thought "Oh God, is this bait the one with the angler on the other end?". It then depends on who is fastest on the draw. Can I react quickly enough with a fast strike to set the hook? Or will the carp blow the bait out and bow-wave away? All nerve tingling, and guaranteed to get the adrenalin flowing.

I enjoy using soft paste baits simply because I am fishing short sessions and will be checking that bait anything from every couple of hours, to every twenty minutes. Much depends on how many small fish are in the water to whittle away the bait to nothing. The boilie was in fact created as a sort of skinned paste bait intended for long durations in the water and to be resistible to the ravages of small fish. If you were asleep all night with a bare hook out you wouldn't be too impressed! My reasoning behind using soft paste baits is that possibly the world and his wife will be using shop-bought boilies. They are uniform in size, and all hard. On a heavily fished water you can often start picking up fish by using something completely different from everyone else.

Following up on this theory, remember when rolling out your loose samples of paste baits, that the boilies you are trying to outfish are all uniform in texture and size. Try rolling very large baits first, and on the first couple of sessions smooth them off by wetting your hands. If you catch regularly, stay with the smooth baits. But if you get finicky feeders, mould the bait into a different shape. Square, pear-shaped, mis-shaped, anything but perfectly round. You can also make a textured paste bait by adding some dry mix after moulding. That too can make a subtle difference. Fished in conjunction with the freeline method, and provided you watch your bobbin indicators all the time, you should pick up the carp. Certainly it has proved a very successful method for me.

Ledgering

This method of fishing is possibly the most popular in use on many carp waters today. It also has the most variations; nowadays some of the rigs are so complicated, that I think the anglers attribute too much intelligence to the carp. To me, ledgering means the addition of a toxic-free weight to counteract any drift or wind factors that preclude me from using the freeline, or to reach a distant swim that I cannot reach without the addition of that weight. I also have to minimise any resistance to a taking fish brought about by the use of that additional lead, and it is here that all the complicated rigs come in.

The easiest to start with is the running ledger rig. You run the mainline of around 8 lb through the eye of the swivel on a lead, stop it about two feet from the end of the line by a plastic ledger stop, then tie on a hook. As easy as that. Bait up, cast out, tighten to the lead and place your bobbin indicator on. When fishing at distance with a straight ledger-rig like this you may have trouble pulling the hook through the bait on the strike. Even with a soft paste bait the elasticity of monofilament line at distance will absorb a lot of the power on the strike. The users of the boilies, and other semi-hard

John Levell returns his double-figure carp. His best session was **four** twenty pounders in a few hours!

Above: The crucian carp in profile. This perfect fish is popular with matchmen and pleasure anglers alike. Free biting and hard scrapping, they can feed right through the heat of a summer's day when all else is hiding in the weedbed.

Left: A perfect miniature. This yearling mirror carp shows how greedy the species can be. However once they get larger, and have been caught a few times they represent a much harder challenge.

Facing page: Saturation livebaits like maggots are still good for smaller carp, although they can attract the attentions of other species. They are best used as an attractor, with a larger hookbait fished in the centre of the swim. Often feeding from other species attracts the interest of a passing carp, which then stops to join in.

The author is known for adapting to almost any fishing situation. When he fished a North Carolina carp lake with Bruce Vaughan, he managed to get a huge number of fish feeding on giant Sugar Puffs at the surface. Presentation was a problem, so he used a fly rod, and fished a single Sugar Puff over thirty yards out. Success was instantaneous, and he took several double-figure carp in a joint haul of over 250lb!

Small carp up to 3lb or so can give the pleasure or match angler some great sport on the pole. Nigel Newport plays a carp hooked at Petersfield's MBK leisure pit.

Carp specialist John Levell, head bailiff of the prolific Somerley Estate water in Hampshire, holds a double-figure carp. Careful management of a carp water enables anglers to catch fish right through the year.

This angler looks delighted with this chunky little mirror carp. Once they get above about 8lb, the carp should still be regarded as a good catch. Don't set your sights too high.

This perfectly scaled common carp fell to a pop-up rig with tiger nut as bait, fished 70 yards out. Captor is Mike Gilbert from West Moors.

baits like nuts and beans found that if the hook was buried in the bait it was virtually impossible to pull the hook through it on the strike. While the boilie had overcome the problem of paste baits being whittled away by nuisance fish, it had created another problem of hooking fish at distance.

Some of these problems were overcome by the use of longer, fast tapered rods that could not only deliver a ledger weight at an incredible distance, but could help drive the hook through the bait. As more anglers fished, so many waters saw the carp being pushed out into the centre of the lake. You had to cast out even further to reach them, so the striking problem was back again. Obviously the hooking rig has to be changed to hit fish at distance when using semi-hard baits, and so the various ledger rigs we see today came into being. Remember that as well as dragging a hook through a bait, you might have to move a weight as well.

Anglers started to rig baits with the hook just nicking the bait so the hookpoint and barb were showing. This originated in the side hooking of the boilie or bean, which was still used in conjunction with the running ledger rig. Again the problems of bobbin drag became apparent on windy days and they created the same drift problems as with freelining, although this time the bait wouldn't be dragged out of position as the lead held it in the swim. But the pull of drift on the line would see the bobbin drag slowly towards the butt ring. Anglers started to ram a piece of foam into a butt ring to pinch the line gently, yet stop the bobbin dragging up.

What then happened was that they started to get rocket-like bites that could drag the rod off the rest if the reel bale arm was left closed. Obviously the smaller twitchy bites couldn't be seen due to the use of the foam, and the fish roared off, hooking itself against the rod. This was the start of what is known as the bolt rig principle. It was found that this bolting act by the carp was accentuated by the use of shorter hooklinks. They shortened down from two or three feet to as close as six inches, and a heavier lead was used. This was not to aid casting, as a single ounce of lead can be cast as far as most swims dictate, but to help drag the hook in the fish, and restrict the line where it was held in place in the butt ring by the piece of foam. The theory behind the idea is that the carp sucks up the bait, moves a few inches, and coming up against the lead, bolts away, with the lead holding the hook in place.

With more and more anglers realising the significance of this advance in rigs came the theory that carp were now wise to the extra lead, and would suck in and blow out a bait several times. The idea now was to tie the bait onto the bend, shank or eye of the hook using a "hair" or very thin piece of 12-oz or 1-lb breaking strain line. Then if the carp sucked a bait in, the bait and hook would disappear into its mouth together, and as the carp tried to blow the bait out again, the hookpoint would catch. Unable to eject the bait properly, it would move off, come up against the 2-oz lead and bolt away hooking itself. Now known as the "hair rig", it is really just a variation of a bolt rig, but with the hook fully exposed as opposed to partially exposed through side hooking. Needle sharp hooks are still required for this rig, and the hookpoint must nick a piece of skin on the carp's first attempt to blow out the bait.

Basically the light 'hair' line of 1 lb or so is tied to the hook, preferably to the bend of the hook, then threaded through the bait using a baiting needle, and prevented from sliding off by using a hair rig stop, or the smallest plastic ledger stop. The length of the hair can be varied from half an inch to two inches, depending on the size of fish you intend catching, and how many you have missed previously. The optimum length would in my opinion be about half an inch. Trial and error is the best way to learn.

Three different types of monkey-climb indicators. The one on the left features weight attachments to combat any sub-surface line drift.

Techniques

Lay out an old ground sheet or canvas liner to sort out your terminal tackle. That way if you drop hooks, swivels etc, they are easily found.

A problem that some anglers have experienced is that the carp, becoming ever more wary, dislikes the stiff nylon of the main line. To combat this, anglers use either dental floss or dacron as a hook link, with the intention of making the carp think it is a piece of weed attached to the bait. Dacron is thicker, but dental floss can be better, as once under water it fluffs up into several different fibres. You can also dye it if you wish — black, brown or green are all food colours. Dental floss can be quite strong, and I regularly use it for sewing up my baits for big-game trolling. Even when dragging a 1-lb fish through the boat's wake for hours on end, I haven't known dental floss to wear out or break up.

You can also use the hair rig in conjunction with the freelined paste baits, but quite honestly with the hook being driven straight through a soft bait into the fish's mouth, I cannot see the need for it. One advantage for freelining might be to make use of the fibrous dental floss as a hooklink if you feel the carp are being finicky due to the stiff nylon mainline.

Using this same system of hook and lead in close proximity, together with the bait and hook attached with a link of fine hair nylon, you can also use the pop-up bait. Initially this was devised as a way of fishing a boilie bait just above any bottom weed that might otherwise obscure the bait from the fish. However, when using a strongly flavoured bait, I feel the carp will root down amongst the weed to locate the source of the smell, and being partially obscured by weed it may not notice the lead and other attachments that might otherwise spook it. That is my theory. On the other hand I also believe that to isolate a bait amongst a carpet of other loose feed must surely increase the chances of that bait being picked up. A bait floating a few inches above all the rest must surely stand out more?

You can make your own pop-up baits simply by fishing a floater, which is buoyant and rises up off the bottom. You can make your own "cake" of floaters, or bake ordinary boilies in an oven for extra time to make them buoyant. Obviously if you mix your own you can beat in plenty of bubbles to the mix before baking, which makes for a better floater. There is no reason why you cannot use a plain or flavoured floater from Chum mixer biscuits, the problem being that all your loose feed is likely to be different to the mixer.

You can also cut the top off, drill a hole, insert a polyball and reglue the top to a shop-bought sinking boilie. Use superglue, but watch your fingers, as it sticks in seconds. All these techniques though, are really no different to the carp anglers of thirty years ago combating the problems of bottom weed obscuring baits by using a balanced paste bait with a crust pad added to buoy it up from the bottom. Things you think are new in fishing really aren't that new at all. The hair rig for example is very similar to the bridle rig used for trolling a livebait for marlin as long as sixty years ago!

Smaller seed baits, can also be fished effectively using this ledger rig. That carp can become preoccupied by small feed is indicated by their natural quest for the tiny bloodworm. For that reason alone mass particles, such as hemp, tares, corn or some cooked nuts which are trying to reproduce the natural feed of bloodworm, are worth introducing. Problems arise however when you want to fish seed baits on a big hook. The same hair and bolt rig process can be used but you can use a few fibres of dental floss, as the hair. This allows several seeds to be superglued to the floss and you can even build up a cluster of seeds.

The advantage of particle saturation is that the carp become so engrossed in feeding that they lose all sense of caution and give you a hell of a confident bite. I feel it best to fish a small cluster of seeds as a pop-up rig by first tying on a piece of buoyant black foam or polystyrene to the hair, then gluing the seeds to that. With a bed of multiple seed baits to choose from, surely an isolated bait, about four inches off the bottom must be taken fairly quickly.

Larger seed and nut baits can be fished as singles, twos or threes, but an occasional mishap that can occur is when the carp get so engrossed in feeding they throw the seeds straight back down their throat and over the pharyngeal teeth. These can chafe through the line resulting in a lost fish. I have some pharyngeal teeth from a 37-lb carp set up by a taxidermist, and I assure you they are quite substantial.

While the average distance for casting with a lead might be under fifty yards, the plastic ledger stop can be safely used. These are fine for medium casting but once you start to give the rod some poke, they can slide down. Two ledger stops fished one against the other will reduce this slippage, but it may be better to tie in a barrel swivel to stop the lead sliding down. This at least allows you to tie on a separate length of hook link, like dacron or dental floss. If distance is the object you can slide a one inch length of flexible tubing from the mainline up to rest on the barrel swivel. Slide a bead up against the tubing, and the lead against that. Then when you cast hard, the tubing compresses to take the initial shock, and doesn't create another weak point near the swivel eye.

A method that is causing some concern at present is the fixed-lead bolt rig, or back-stopping, which creates the same problem. Some anglers found they got a better hook-up rate when they clipped or fixed the lead directly to the swivel, or mainline. But instead of the fish pulling against the resistance of the foam in the butt ring, they banged straight into the lead which spooked them and pulled the hook in. Unfortunately any carp that was accidentally broken off and swam into a tangle of thick weed or branches, was likely to get the lead snapped and so be tethered until it died. Some clubs have now banned the use of the fixed lead.

The same goes for back-stopping, which meant having a fixed point, maybe a ledger stop, a few feet up the mainline from the hook. The carp took the bait, but could move several feet before banging up against the back-stop. Again, this rig caught plenty of fish, but if any breakage occurred above the back-stop, that carp would be towing the lead around until it got snagged up and died.

With a billowy hook length like dental floss, there can be problems of tangles when the hook link twists around the mainline, offering resistance to a taking fish. For that reason a length of tubing keeps the hooklink from tangling with the lead on the cast. The system works and you can buy a range of different anti-tangle rigs from most leading tackle shops. They can be adapted for either hard or weedy bottoms, and even offer semi-fixed rigs that should fall free from the fish should an unexpected breakage occur. I personally do not use them much, but then I am usually sitting by my rods for shorter periods of time, and will be casting out several times over a session of a few hours anyway.

Having dealt with the ledger rigs available, you will have noticed that all the aforementioned rigs deal with the hook link hanging below the lead. In fact you can use a paternoster rig, which entails the lead being tied on a link below the hook. The mainline runs through the top swivel to indicate a resistance-free bite, and if a breakage occurs, the lead and link falls free from the fish. You also have the option to fish the link with the lead attached as a weak link that breaks if the lead becomes snagged, thus allowing you to fight the fish unhindered.

When using a heavy lead for distance casting and the bottom is known to be silty, or covered with soft bottom weed you obviously fish the pop-up bait rig on a hair. But what do you do to stop the lead sinking into the mud/weed and the swivel becoming clogged, thus giving undue resistance to a taking carp? That problem came up years ago and was solved by gluing a balsa body over the top of an Arseley bomb. That held the lead up vertically when it hit the bottom, and allowed the swivel to remain clear of the weed. I also have added an extension of several inches to my bombs, much like the stainless steel wire "tail" we use when distance beach casting. This tail is to maintain stable aerodynamics on the cast and prevent the lead wobbling about. However it can be fitted with a swivel which is then held in place by a short length of flexible tubing slid up over half the length of the barrel swivel. Yet another problem is solved!

If you want to fish in holes in the weedbeds, and remember the leaves on the surface cover a larger area than the stems under water, tie up the lead in a parcel using strips of PVA that dissolve in the water. Alternatively you can put the whole rig, bait and all into a tiny P.V.A. bag and cast it out. This allows you to fish even the weediest swim, and of course on hot, bright days this could well be where the carp are.

Floater Fishing

This is my favourite method of taking carp. You have the visual excitement, all the thrill of the stalking, and you get to learn a great deal about the carp's reaction to different baits. The simplest method is to freeline a floating bait in front of a cruising fish. Easier said than done, as the first problem lies in finding the feeding carp. The traditional bait of early carping was a piece of crust. Hook it on, dunk it once to absorb casting weight and cast out. So simple it seems ridiculous, but I still use it and the carp still take it. Except now I carry an atomizer of flavouring that I spray it with after first dunking it in the water.

You can also make up your own cake of floater mix at home adding as many different flavourings and colourings as take your fancy. You can use circular or square pieces cut from the cake, or simply break off an uneven piece if you think the carp are a bit canny about uniformly shaped baits. You can also buy shop-supplied floaters, which are the easiest to use. But the best, by way of money has to be the cat or dog food mixers. Simply soak them in water, strain off into a plastic bag, pour in a capful of the required flavouring, shake about, and leave to swell up and absorb the flavouring. You can freeze it down with no apparent ill effects, and for scattering around they represent a minimum outlay in cost. If the gulls eat them, no problem, a big sack from the Cash and Carry costs only a few pounds. Never catapult them too far out unless the wind is in your face, otherwise they may drift out of casting range before they get taken by carp. For freelining alone you will be restricted for casting weight.

Additional weights can be used in the shape of a shop-bought controller, which comes in various sizes. Or you can make your own controller by moulding a piece of green Flotabait around a two-inch length of tubing, like biro tube. It can be stopped by a swivel and the hooklink, or fished as a permanent fixture by plugging with a ledger stop. This is pretty good for distance casting in rough or ripply water. For fishing medium range in still conditions I simply pinch a piece of Flotabait, about the size of my thumbnail around a permanently fixed plastic ledger stop about two feet or more from the Chum mixer. If a ripple does spring up and you aren't quite sure whether to strike as your floater is obscured, you can wait for the Flotabait to tweak or disappear. It really is quite buoyant.

You can always make your own controllers by cutting cylinders of balsa wood, inserting a biro tube, or fixing a wire through the centre, housing a swivel through which the line is passed. You can also add lead within the base of the balsa body to cock the controller like a float. Stop it from sliding down to the floater by using a plastic ledger stop. You could also use a swan shot pinched lightly on the mainline, above the ledger stop as casting weight, then counterbalance this by moulding the green Flotabait over the top. I have heard of floaters being fished on a hair rig, but quite honestly cannot really see the point as any floater you are likely to be using can have a hook driven through it on the strike. Also where the hair is designed to stop a carp blowing the bait in and out of its mouth, you will have the added advantage of seeing the take visually. Therefore you can strike immediately. Always pause a second before striking to allow the carp to turn down with the bait.

If you decide on controllers, make sure you purchase several different weights and sizes. There are some about that lie flat, while others cock like a normal float. Depending on the length of hook link you are using, and the clarity of water, they will be visible to the carp. I make the suggestion that you repaint the lower half of the cocking float the same colour as the environment in which you are fishing it. If close to lilies a bottle green base will blend in nicely. If it rests against rush stems a light brown would be better. It may be useful to carry a small box of various colours and sizes of controllers for all situations you are likely to encounter.

For the freelined floater, a floating hooklink or mainline will silhouette itself against the backdrop of sky, varying on the cloud situation. It is possible that carp that boil away from a floater see this silhouette. Try degreasing the hooklink with detergent, and you may get a more positive take.

For a drifting floater, where you are working it down a swim with either surface drift or breeze, it is possible to keep the line from the hook out of the water completely using a suspender. This is a round polyball float with a long plastic tube and balance weight that to all intents and purposes looks like a baby fishing rod. It merely holds the last few inches of line off the water, so only the bait is touching, hung vertically from the tiny "rod". This works well initially, but carp soon learn to associate the polyball with a pain in the mouth! Repaint the polyball like the controllers to blend in with any natural surroundings.

The other way to stop the fish seeing the line when you want to anchor a floater in one position, but also keep the line to the bait off the water, is to use a long rod like a beach caster, cast out with a 2-oz lead, heavy pike float, and suspend the hooklink about three feet from the pike float. The lead holds everything in position, and the beach caster keeps the line clear of the water. You could also cast into a bush or tree on the opposite bank with the beach caster, then using a second rod with a sliding link, run your floater down the beach caster line, which is kept taut, letting out line until the floater touches the surface. I don't like this method very much as you may break off the beach caster line in the bush, which is not conducive to keeping the bird watchers happy. If you use a heavy line to avoid breakage you could tear off branches from trees and bushes. However I mention it as another successful method of catching carp.

Baits

The world of baits used for catching carp can become even more bizarre than the rigs, and I imagine an entire book could be given to the subject. Anglers have amazing minds. They conjure up unbelievable recipes for carp in the belief that the carp will be impressed. In fact the carp takes a bait because it is hungry, nothing more. The more times they are caught, the more discerning they become about what they eat and when.

Start with the basics if the water you are fishing is comparatively easy. I would advise starting with a venue that is not renowned for its monster catches, but for the numbers of small to medium range fish it has; it will therefore have received less angling attention. Also the larger head of fish will mean competition is greater for food items, and you are more likely to hit a fish. Experience even with

An 18 pounder from a hard fished day-ticket water in Surrey puts a smile on the author's face. On this water a double-figure fish is unusual, and perseverance with outsize baits proved the carp's downfall.

small carp will stand you in good stead for catching the bigger specimens.

Bread

Bread is still the most simple bait to use. An uncut loaf is best as it gives you soft white flake which you use for slow sinking baits on the bottom, and crust which is great for surface fishing. A carp will take an incredible chunk of crust, as large as a matchbox sometimes, so don't be frightened into using small pieces. Hook once through the soft side and into the crust, then turn the hook over and bring the point back through the crust to the white side. Dunk in the water for a second or two to absorb water and give you casting weight, and cast out. You will probably only get one cast from it, as it flies off when waterlogged. If you use flake remember to take a small atomiser of flavouring with you. Anoint your flake after squeezing around the hook and you could induce that extra fish or two.

Worms

As far as I am concerned, for carp you need use nothing smaller than the biggest, strangling great lobworm you can find. Ledgered on the bottom they are great; just snap off a tiny portion of tail to let the body juices work out. If you have a silty, or weedy lakebed, make a pop-up bait from him by injecting with air. I have used this technique in Arkansas in the States while fishing for river rainbows over heavy weedbeds — and I can vouch it works a treat.

Casters

One of the best baits for small to medium carp, casters probably come under the heading of particle baits, but as they require no mixing or cooking I include them here. Thread as many as a dozen casters onto a strong, fine wire hook and add plenty of loose feed with a little groundbait. The use of several casters on the hook should minimise attention from unwanted species.

Go Fishing for Carp

Maggots

The largest, home-bred gozzers are the best, but failing that try straight whites, again feeding with groundbait. Work ten or fifteen maggots onto a size two carp hook and you should get the carp, not the smaller roach and rudd. Unfortunately maggots, along with worms, prove highly attractive to eels after dark!

Paste Baits

There are some weird recipes for paste baits. Years ago you made a paste up from flour and water and simply flavoured it with sugar, honey, molasses or aniseed. That now sounds terribly dated, but find a water where the carp have yet to receive angler attention and they will work. Of those used most frequently today, I shall mention just one base to start with as I believe it is the best, and I have caught enough fish with it, including bags over 100 lb and 20-lb-plus fish so that I know it works.

Trout in rearing ponds have to be fed a very high protein diet to boost their growth rate. This is done with trout pellets — a ground and then compacted protein feed — fed dry. Made basically from fish meal, the carp love it, as do tench and bream; it is also easy to use. On its own it is good; as a base for other additives it is even better. All you need do is scald the required bucket of pellets for your session with boiling water for about 25 seconds. Strain off immediately, allow to cool, then squeeze until pliable. The mixture gets sticky, so keep your hands wet when mixing it up. You can add colourings and flavourings to suit. Best flavours I have found are honey/creme, freshwater mussel or strawberry. Your local tackle dealer will carry a huge selection, more than enough to keep you going for the first season. Make a large quantity, squeeze it into blocks, cling film it then put it in the freezer for later use. That way you only get gunked up once for several sessions of fishing. When you're ready to use it, you can make it into large balls, tiny pellets, make it smooth or rough textured, shaped or rough. A lot of anglers think the simple paste bait is finished, but nobody has told the carp yet as I can still catch them on it!

Baits

Seed Baits

The easiest seed bait of all to use is sweetcorn. Purchased ready cooked, you can fish a single, double or treble-grain hookbait, threading the grains straight onto the hook or using the hair rig. Or you can really go for it and thread a dozen grains over the hook shank, and up the line in what we call a "necklace". You can buy tins, but please open the tin at home and transfer the contents into a plastic bait container. There really is no excuse for dumping dangerous cans in the bushes. Or you can get better value for money by buying a big bag of frozen corn, and dividing it up into several smaller bags. Corn has a reputation for going sour within a day in the summer, so throw in what you don't use. Red is one of the best colours to use on it. I dislike flavouring corn though as it has a distinctive flavour of its own and there's no need therefore to change it.

Boilies

This has to be the most revolutionary new bait for carp. Boilies originated from the need of anglers to form a protective skin over a paste bait, to avoid it being nibbled away when left in the water for long periods. A spell in boiling water would put this skin on them, but it wasn't long before the commercial bait suppliers saw an opening in the market and began making 'boilies' for anglers who had neither time nor inclination to spend time slaving over a hot stove in the kitchen! More details on the manufacture of boilies, (as well as many other baits) can be found in the *Graeme Pullen Guide to Freshwater Fishing Baits.*

With the shop-bought boilie, you just walk in to your tackle dealer and choose the required flavour and colour you want, with the option on buying either frozen or shelf-life baits. The range of flavourings and colouring is awe inspiring, and more than adequate for even the most pernickety carp. All these boilies come in two sizes: standard and mini. Generally you may find it best to lay a carpet of mini boilies in the swim to induce feeding, then fish a standard-size boilie over the top. The alternative is to make up your

The most convenient carp bait in use today, boilie baits can be bought either from the tackle shop shelf or freezer in a wide variety of colours and flavours.

own boilies, which gives you the advantage of not only producing much bigger baits, but to alter the shape of them. Basically you buy your base mix, put in eggs, flavourings and colourings to suit and cook up at home. You can put a skin on them by boiling. Although very time consuming, you can at least control the amount of flavouring you put in. Take note that too much colouring or flavouring will actually repel fish. Never think the more you put in the better the bait will be. You really just need a hint of flavour, just enough to make the fish pick up the bait. Put on a hair rig, the carp should be as good as yours. It is cheaper to make up your own boilies, and of course, a well-stocked tackle shop can offer you a wide choice of additives.

Nuts and Seeds

Probably one of the more controversial baits because when fed too heavily, and either presented unhooked or partially cooked they have been found to kill carp. Many clubs have banned their use because of this. Although a carp has enormous pharyngeal throat teeth to crunch up things, they can digest soft cooked nuts more easily. Some of the more successful nuts are tigers, cashew, peanuts, walnuts and maples. Of the seeds, as they are called, kidney beans, chic peas, broad beans, and even baked beans are good. Seeds absorb colours and flavours much better than nuts and are softer baits so therefore safer to use.

The harder nuts need to be boiled for a considerable time. Better to soak them overnight first in a bucket of cold water, then cook them the next day. Some nuts may take an hour to cook, and you need to keep a watchful eye on the saucepan to ensure it doesn't boil dry. A pressure cooker will shorten the cooking time, but soaking overnight usually helps anyway. You can freeze them down after cooking for later use, but some of the flavourings you may add will be reduced by this. All nuts are better fished on hair rigs in case the hooks turn into the bait when striking. Check with your angling club or day ticket as to which nuts, if any, are banned. I wouldn't be surprised if more nuts are banned in the future. Soft beans and peas are obviously perfectly alright when fished in moderation.

Floaters

These can be as simple as a crust of bread, or a complex "cake" mixed up at home from any of the base mixes, colourings and flavourings obtained from your tackle shop. By far the cheapest are the dog and cat food "mixer" type of biscuits, that need only be soaked for ten minutes, then drained off and a lid put on the container, to absorb moisture. I never bother with colouring, but it may pay dividends to tip the soaked mixer biscuits into a plastic bag, add a capful of your chosen flavouring, then blow up the bag and roll the contents around to ensure the flavouring is properly absorbed. Soak up a large batch, then put them into smaller bags and freeze them for later use.

Without going into the complex world of bait additives, why not try a few of the following — you might get a few giggles from other carp anglers, but watch the smile drain from their faces when you slide the net under a carp! Luncheon meat, either tinned or in a block from the cold meat counter of the supermarket is good, as is cheese, an excellent, little-used bait. Try mixing a strong cheese additive to fine white groundbait, mix into large balls, throw out, then fish a ball of English Cheddar over the top. Loose feeding with 5 lb of cheese is damned expensive, but groundbait and cheese additive is not. Sausage meats can be moulded into balls and fished as freeline baits over a carpet of sweetcorn. It works, so never knock it until you have tried it . . . several times.

Finally, try some of the fishy tinned catfoods. Mix them into a

You do not need a big carp to be happy. Graham Earle looks delighted with this Wiltshire carp that he caught on floating crust, on directions from the author.

paste with fine white groundbait, and roll into large balls, suitable for a size 2 hook. They were highly successful fifteen years ago, and with hardly anybody using them today, can still be productive. They smell a bit when mixing up, but that's why the carp love them.

Tackle

I have no intention of listing each and every item of tackle available to the dedicated carp angler. The range is enormous and eventually you will end up owning several rods, reels and a wealth of supplementary items. To catch carp on a prolific water all you need is a rod, reel, line, hooks, bait and landing net.

Here are some of the better **rods** at the top end of the range that

No more driving rod rests into hard ground. The modern carp angler has the opportunity of using this fully adjustable stainless steel rest outfit, complete with monkey-climb indicators. Price — around £175!

are certainly worth looking at: the 12-foot long-distance rod made by Century Composites; the Armelite $2\frac{1}{4}$ lb test curve with a line range of 7/15 lb; the Drennan 12-foot $2\frac{1}{2}$ lb test curve model which will cast easily from 50 to 120 yards, depending on the lead and conditions; the Armelite 12-foot, 2-lb test curve for medium-range work of 20/80 yards; (there are also similar models in both Sportex and Drennan) for close range work like margin fishing, a 12-foot rod with a $1\frac{3}{4}$-lb test curve is ideal — try Armelite, Sportex and Drennan.

On cheaper rods you can catch plenty of fish with the long-range 12-foot Silstar, Ryobi and Normark rods. It may be better for a beginner to buy these cheaper rods in case he can't get on with carping. Try looking at the new Powerloop from Shimano. Another tip is that a long-range rod will be fast taper and great for casting and striking, but it can be very easy to overpower a carp at close range and break him off. Take it easy when the fish gets close by the net. In contrast, a margin rod will be slow taper, sloppy, and bend round easily on the strike. No good for hook setting at long range, but very forgiving under pressure and at close quarters. Think of the style of fishing you will be doing before you buy.

For **reels,** the best must be made by Shimano. For your average style of carping, possibly with bolt-rigs at the forefront, one of the best is the Baitrunner series. For long range work try the BTR-GT-3500 and 4500 which have enormous line capacities and a special feature in the shape of a rear tension adjuster. This does the same job as a piece of foam jammed in the butt ring; a simple flick, and you are on preset strike drag. Also in the long-range bracket is their Biomaster, the 4000 taking up to 270 yards of 12-lb test line. For those who still like the stern drag feature, there is the Aerlex GTR with ultra smooth drag. Both models feature a wide, oscillating spool for perfect line lay, resulting in longer casts.

Cheaper Shimanos come in the shape of the Carbomatic range, with stern drags and preset strike feature. For long range the CBM-GT-400 is used, with the CBM-GT 3000 used for medium and close-range work. There are also very good reels available from Ryobi Masterline, perfectly adequate for the beginner, and all competitively priced.

Tackle

Three of the best reels from the Shimano stable. On the left, the Shimano Baitrunner 3500 GT. Centre is a Shimano 5000 Biomaster, with twin oscillating spool. On the right, a Shimano 3000X.

Other items such as **hooks** are very much down to the individual. I personally like the Jack Hilton range available from Partridge of Redditch. In fact Partridge can offer a huge range of hooks, right down to specialist hair rig hooks and hair rig baiting needles. For smaller carp, up to double figures, the specialist hooks by Partridge are great. Also look out for the Drennan Boilie hooks, and the Kevin Nash Sprite hooks.

On the subject of **lines,** there are three worth looking at. In heavier ranges for hit-and-hold tactics I use the American Ande 12-lb Premium line. It is limp and soft, yet takes a lot of punishment at maximum pressure. For smaller lines 5/12 lb Maxima Chameleon and Sylcast in the Sorrel colour are most popular. Maxima seems to me virtually invisible under water, and Sylcast has tremendous durability, great for long-range work.

The best **nets** seem to be the Gardner 36 and 42-inch models. You can slot any carp from British waters in one of these. In fact if you get a five pounder it may take you a while to find it! Big nets are better than ones that are too small! Of the other pieces of **misc-ellaneous** equipment, if you want to keep a carp overnight for a

Landing nets should be the largest you can find. This version has a large mesh over most of its area so you can sweep it through the water, but a fine mesh in the bottom, to avoid damaging the fish.

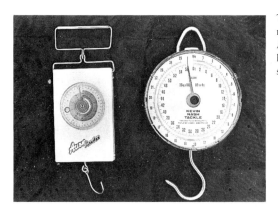

The two best scales on the market. On the left are the Avon scales, on the right the heavier duty Kevin Nash scales, both are excellent.

daytime photograph, the Kevin Nash **sacks** are good; available in standard, extra large and king size. To weigh your fish you want either a set of Kevin Nash dial **scales** weighing to 56 lb in one ounce divisions, or the Avon Dial scales weighing to 40 lb in one ounce divisions. Make sure you use a **weigh sling** for the carp. You might also want to invest in an **unhooking mat,** which also avoids damage to the fish if you have landed him on gravel, or hard ground. E.T. and Kevin Nash supply models.

If you night fish you need a large **brolly,** where allowed, a **bivouac cover** to go over the top, a **bed, chair, sleeping bag,** etc. Once you start thinking of comfort on overnight and extended sessions you really start to enter the world of the camper. Many items available at camping stores will prove useful on long sessions, but I honestly only see the need for a bivvy on autumn and winter nights. You need **forceps, leads, hair rigs, non-tangle rigs, cameras** and so many auxiliary items that you begin to wonder if your bank manager will turn up at your swim. Of course **bite indicators** really are required, even if you sit awake by the rods like me. Then you can at least glance away and not miss the pee-peep of a bite. Optonics are the best, and ideal for other stillwater species as well.

Three types of modern alarms for bite indication. On the left, the Bitech Viper, with a volume and tone control, also suitable for slack line bites. Centre, is a Super Compact Optonic with volume and tone control, plus a latching L.E.D. which allows the light indication to register for fifteen seconds after the bite. You can also get an extension box with this. On the right, the standard Optonic sensor with audible and visual system.

Go Fishing for Carp

So there you have a guide to catching the carp. If you enjoy fishing a very hard water with just a few fish in it then look to other books on the subject, far more detailed than mine. But if you just want to feel that surge of power as a carp takes the bait, then aim for small to middle of the road fish. A double figure carp is still a good fish. A twenty pounder a really good fish, and a thirty something to dream about. And if you just want fun without resorting to expensive outlays and all-night sessions try waters where there are plenty of carp from 3 lb up to double figures. They offer the cream of our carp sport. From here, if you want, you can go on and progress to the bigger fish. Meanwhile appreciate the carp for what it is — possibly our hardest scrapping stillwater fish, and almost our national species!

The Future of Carp Fishing

I would be the first to say that any changes regarding new species, whether strains introduced or British hybridisations, should be taken seriously. I am sure the grass carp will enter the carp scene eventually, whether it is used as a means of weed control that obviates the requirement for chemicals, or it is simply stocked for its novelty value. We have already seen the coming and going of hybrids throughout the trout world where the cheetah, tiger, and the more recognisable brook trout were popular with fishermen simply because they were something different. British records were set up and broken quite regularly as fisheries vied for the chance of publicity. Then, almost as suddenly as they appeared, they vanished. The fish farms stopped cross-breeding and remained with just browns and rainbows, and I imagine things will stay that way for quite some time.

In the carp world however, I think there is already a boom under way, which will see not only venues limited to carp only, but more intensive fish farming for the species as a means of supplying the fishing clubs. The requirement of instant big carp I have mentioned previously, but I feel this will be followed by the need of anglers to catch the rarer species. I myself am a dedicated marlin fisherman, hunting this species of billfish over the three warm oceans, I want to catch all eight species, but so far have taken five — catching the broadbill, mediterranean shortbill spearfish, and the rarer longbill

103

spearfish may be almost impossible.

I feel the carp angler will not be content to "collect" his list of big common, leather, mirror, saddleback, linear, grass and crucian carp for long. He will want to say he has caught them all, and to that end I put the most expensive carp of all on their list — the Koi carp. Sounds impossible. Well, if you were a dedicated carp fisherman, who had landed all the main types, how much would you be prepared to pay to add a big Koi carp to your list? I know a Mediterranean shortbill spearfish would command a special price if I had a means of catching one but in the open oceans of the world nature must take its course — with carp fishing however the species can simply be bred.

There are many carp farms over the country, and they supply the ornamental fish pond enthusiast with all manner of small Kois. They are very, VERY, expensive, and you may think you need to fish in a private ornamental pond to stand a chance of catching one. Not so, for a few waters already have them stocked. In this respect I can claim a first as I took a small one from a Wiltshire trout lake, and to give it even more "cult" status, I took it on a fly rod!

To give you a bit of an insight into the Koi carp world I paid a visit to a trout fishery in Sussex that also bred on Kois. Here they get through about one million trout and carp each year, although the Kois demand more attention because of their high unit value. This species first came into Britain in any quantity around 1955 from Japan, and strangely, they were not an instant success. The goldfish boom was on then, and it took several years for the Koi to achieve their exclusive status in the ponds and lakes. Then suddenly they became "fashionable".

A Koi in tip-top condition can fetch as much as £1 for a one to two inch fish, up to, and over, £30 for larger specimens. Much depends on the life expectancy, and an expensive Koi can be between 17 and 25 years of age. The brood fish are obviously highly prized for the stock they can produce, and may reach the top prices. The colour toning and individual markings draw the attention of the true collector. The female lays the eggs, many of which may not be fertile if conditions are not correct, using one female to three males. Unlike the trout, the Koi is not hand-stripped of eggs, but

The Future of Carp Fishing

A double figure koi carp being hand fed. This may be the latest "cult" species for the serious carp angler.

allowed to spawn naturally on special spawning ropes sunk below the surface of the water.

The adult fish are removed after spawning, and the eggs allowed to remain undisturbed in the stock pond for up to six days before completion of hatching. Some may hatch as early as two days after laying if the temperature range is constant between 75 and 80 degrees fahrenheit. Once hatched, they are left to feed on the contents of their egg sacks for a further couple of days, then their diet consists of live brine shrimp. These brine shrimps are bred on site, with some fifty million eggs a week produced. The feed is then changed to a powdered protein, and the fry stay in this stable environment for four weeks. The next stage is to remove them to a concrete raceway system, where they are fed on Infersoria, a plank-tonic feed, and Daphnia, a water flea. They are left until six to nine weeks old, then moved into the carp lakes and fed on a regular diet of high-protein trout pellet feed.

To wholesale or retail Koi carp you need a big display area for potential customers to view the fish. You also need backup services and installations, and the risk factor of such a high priced live commodity being stolen is considerable. A lot of the Koi collectors buy for the increased revenue of growing on a fish, especially if that fish has the desired tonal colour range, and rare black markings.

To produce the best fish, the stock ponds are put in what is known as a poly-tunnel. This is a metal arched framework covered with heavy duty polythene that stabilises water temperatures between that all important 75/80°F. They look much like a large commercial greenhouse. Compared to carp held outside, with the constant heat of the poly-tunnel the Koi has three times the growth rate. Pride of place in the Sussex operation is a Koi called "Mary Rose". Built like the proverbial battleship, this huge Koi has beautiful markings and has a value in excess of £7000! And if she keeps growing, the price will go even higher.

This Koi operation also supplies fishing clubs with standard mirror carp up to 20 lb in weight, which cost several hundred pounds. The commons may command an even higher price, although small stock fish from half a pound to a pound in weight

A "poly-tunnel", used in the commercial carp rearing of koi to maintain a constant temperature.

usually go for about £2.50 to £3. Crucians are not grown commercially, as they are slow growers, and like the brown trout, work out too expensive in feed and manpower hours per fish. A few farms do try to supply them. If your intention is to add another notch to your rod butt, then look in the future to selected carp lakes, where syndicates offer big fish, and may have the finance among members to include one or two Koi carp to spice up things. And if you really want the ultimate in one-upmanship, how about catching a cross between a Koi and a mirror. They are being bred at present, and are called "Ghost" Kois.

All this is in the future — but that may only be a few years away.

GO FISHING FOR

GO FISHING FOR
TROUT
GRAEME PULLEN

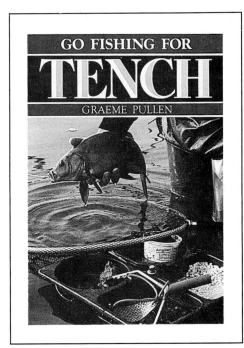

GO FISHING FOR
TENCH
GRAEME PULLEN

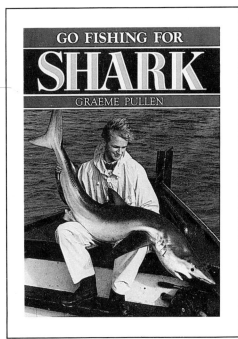

GO FISHING FOR
SHARK
GRAEME PULLEN

GO FISHING FOR
COD
GRAEME PULLEN

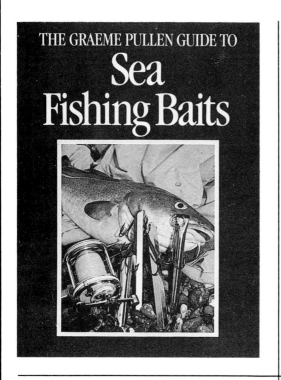
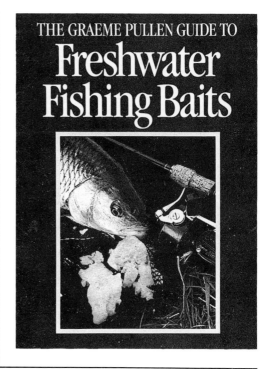